How to Live Your Dreams

Find a Tree and Get Started

DANIEL ARMSTRONG

How to Live Your Dreams

Find a Tree and Get Started

How to Live Your Dreams
Find a Tree and Get Started
by Daniel Armstrong

© **Copyright 2014**
Revised Edition

For inquiries and to order additional copies, please contact:
Find A Tree
6230 Wilshire Boulevard #45
Los Angeles, California 90048-5104
Telephone: 1-866-Find-A-Tree (346-3287)
E-Mail: info@FindATree.com
Internet: FindATree.com
Facebook: Facebook.com/FindATree

Front cover painting by Omari Armstrong (age 14)

ISBN: 978-0-9906388-0-3
eBook ISBN: 978-0-9906388-1-0

Publisher's Cataloging-In-Publication Data
(Prepared by The Donohue Group, Inc.)

Armstrong, Daniel, 1963-
How to live your dreams : find a tree and get started / Daniel Armstrong. -- Revised edition.

pages : illustrations ; cm

Issued also as an ebook.
ISBN: 978-0-9906388-0-3

1. Armstrong, Daniel, 1963- 2. Goal (Psychology) 3. Self-actualization (Psychology) 4. Success--Psychological aspects. I. Title.

BF505.G6 A76 2014

158.1

DEDICATION

For Mom and Dad—Marie and Reginald Armstrong.

Thank you for encouraging me to explore life and to pursue my dreams.

IN MEMORIAM

Dr. Fred A. Kennedy

Educator, humanitarian, father, friend.

Also Written by Daniel Armstrong

Live Your Dreams Now:
Read About It! Write About It! And Do Something!
(A Youth Workbook)

Unlock Students' Potential:
The Blueprint for Motivating Students to Achieve

CONTENTS

Foreword   11

Preface   13

Introduction   17

PART ONE: How to Live Your Dreams

Chapter 1: Yes, You Can Live Your Dream   21

The Find A Tree Principles   26

Chapter 2: Identify What You Are Passionate About,   27
Your Interests, Talents, and Your Gifts

Chapter 3: Determine Your Dream: Find a Tree   37
and Get Started

Chapter 4: Explore Life   41

Chapter 5: Nurture Your Dream with Knowledge   51

Chapter 6: Empower Yourself   57

Chapter 7: Be Willing to March into Hell   59

Chapter 8: Build the Trust of Others   63

Chapter 9: Embrace Struggle   67

Chapter 10: Sometimes You Just Have to Have Faith   75

Chapter 11: Create Opportunities through Service   85

Chapter 12: Value People   87

Chapter 13: Plan, Prioritize, and Manage Your Time   97

Chapter 14: Distinguish Yourself with Excellence   103

Chapter 15: Understand the Process: From a Seed to a Tree   107

Chapter 16: Tap into Your Creative Genius   109

Chapter 17: You Will Achieve What You Expect and Try   111

Chapter 18: Lead Yourself   117

Chapter 19: Start a Business   129

Chapter 20: Work in Harmony with Universal Law
(There Is No Santa Claus)   139

Chapter 21: Where Do We Go from Here?   145

Chapter 22: Conclusion: Building a Better World   155

They Found Their Tree

- No Tree? Use the Stairs — The Otha Johnson III Story

- $25 and a Dream of Going to Africa — by Anita White

- From Lock-up to Beverly Hills — The Darwin Ramirez Story

- Soul 2 Sole: International Bridge of Goodwill — by Lauren Dorsey

- Scoring Points with NBA Executives — by Mathew Fournier

PART TWO: The Workbook

Section 1: The Seed: Finding Your Tree

1. Your Story   162

2. Talents and Interests   170

3. Contribution and Service   174

4. Your Dream   175

5. Vision and Mission Statements   176

6. Research, Information, and Knowledge   178

7. Character   179

8. Sacrifice, Focus, and Priorities   179

9. Faith, Obstacles, and Creativity   180

10. Struggle, Determination, and Starting Small   181

Section 2: The Trunk: Taking Action

1. Your Plan of Action   186

2. Year-Long and Monthly Goals   188

3. Implementation Steps   190

4. Time Management   191

5. Resources   196

Section 3: The Branches: Building Your Dream

1. Teamwork   198

2. Human Relations   198

3. Health   199

4. Organization and Leadership   203

5. Excellence   204

6. Music and Literature   205

7. International Relations   206

Section 4: The Fruit: Starting Your Business

1. Economics   210

2. Money   210

3. Customers and Market Research   211

4. Service and Products   212

5. Start-Up and the Law   212

6. Marketing   213

7. Finance and Accounting   215

8. Human Resources   216

FOREWORD

I credit the Find A Tree program with the amazing accomplishments of the young men I met at the Fred C. Nelles Youth Correctional Facility. These young men have committed serious crimes and lost faith in themselves and the world. If the Find A Tree program can turn them around, then it is something that has a place in the life of any young person. The impact of Find A Tree on the way young people see themselves and how they interact in the world is an element that is sorely missing in the lives of today's youth. Many do not understand how to take control of their own lives, set goals, and then realize those dreams or goals.

I wholeheartedly recommend Find A Tree to anyone who is looking for a way to motivate and mobilize young people to achieve.

Jaleesa Hazzard
Former Executive Director
Y.E.S. to Jobs
Beverly Hills, California

PREFACE

Do not look at this as just a book.

Consider this as a mirror—one meant to reflect the greatness lying inside of you.

Consider this as a match—one meant to ignite your passion and spirit.

Consider this as a vessel—one meant to put you on a course toward your dreams.

When I first drafted *How to Live Your Dreams: Find a Tree and Get Started,* I did so with the mission of improving the lives of others through the gift of empowerment, guidance, and inspiration. Now, with each word you read, my dream is being actualized and my purpose is being fulfilled.

Disregard my dream for a moment. I hope what you'll find as you read on is that you too will bring your aspirations to fruition by identifying them, and acting with a sense of urgency in pursuing your goals.

How to Live Your Dreams won't change your circumstances, but it will change how you view and navigate them in order to make real progress in your life. The lessons and anecdotes inside are meant to challenge how you think, inspire self-reflection, spark action, and provide you with the encouragement necessary to accomplish greatness.

Eliminating excuses, creating opportunities, and fostering a shift in thinking: I've committed my life to helping others achieve these things.

An ancient Chinese proverb states, "The best time to plant a tree was twenty years ago. The second best time is now." Take a moment to think about that, and then read on…to find *your* tree and get started *today*.

Daniel Armstrong
Los Angeles, California

"It is not the critic who counts; not the man who points out how the strong man stumbles, or where the doer of deeds could have done them better. The credit belongs to the man who is actually in the arena, whose face is marred by dust and sweat and blood; who strives valiantly; who errs, who comes short again and again, because there is no effort without error and shortcoming; but who does actually strive to do the deeds; who knows great enthusiasms, the great devotions; who spends himself in a worthy cause; who at the best knows in the end the triumph of high achievement, and who at the worst, if he fails, at least fails while daring greatly, so that his place shall never be with those cold and timid souls who neither know victory nor defeat."

—THEODORE ROOSEVELT

INTRODUCTION

In 1994, I spent six months in Accra, the capital of Ghana, assisting in the organization of an international conference hosted by this West African nation's government. Despite an often hectic work schedule, I always made a point to leave the office by mid-afternoon to play and teach basketball in a section of Accra called Nima. There, young men and women gathered every day on the basketball court of a local church. This court had large cracks in its cement and backboards that shook after every shot. The basketballs were worn thin. Play was rough and competitive, but friendly.

These players, just like youngsters on every playground in America, dreamed of playing pro ball despite their lack of formal training. They dreamed of going to the United States to play in the NBA.

Over the course of time, I was welcomed into this fraternity of young athletes. Through our conversations after practice, I had a chance to see the world from their perspective and learn more about them as individuals. I was surprised that few had dreams other than to leave Ghana. With little education and even less money, obtaining a visa to travel would be difficult for them. Most had unique skills or talents, whether it was fixing a car engine, weaving kente cloth (the national fabric of Ghana), or working with computers. Yet, many did nothing to develop these talents. They spent most days playing basketball in the afternoon and wishing they could go to America.

Some areas of Accra have beautiful homes with manicured lawns. Like many modern cities, there are traffic jams and twenty-story buildings. Nima, however, is notorious for being one of Accra's poorest sections. Many residents live in homes that have no indoor plumbing. Some have roofs that appear to be no more than tin sheets. At that time, before cell phones became commonplace, few had phones in their homes, a job to go to, or a car to drive.

Ghanaians themselves would laugh when I told them that I considered Nima to be my home when in that country. They felt it inconceivable that I would even want to visit that area of town.

I returned to Ghana in 1997 to pursue business and development projects and to find my friends in the Nima community. This time I was determined to help these young people not only with their basketball defense and jump shots, but also to help them transform their lives and develop their community.

The first challenge was to help the young people of Nima recognize and value their individual talents and gifts, as these could serve as the means to transform their wretched living conditions into a community that other Ghanaians would respect.

I asked all the young people to identify what they would dream of doing in life, based on what they love to do. After identifying their interests, I let them know that together we would develop a project or program to help put them on the path toward realizing those dreams. The goal of these projects would be to give their lives purpose and focus, and to change their living conditions.

Twin brothers, Jonas and Jonathan Atingbui, who were seventeen years old, said they loved to teach and wanted to start a school. "Great," I said. The brothers indicated that they would need money to rent a facility. I was working with limited resources, so I advised them, "Just find a tree and get started." They did. Soon Jonas and Jonathan had 50 and then 100 students coming throughout the day to their school under the tree. They began charging a small weekly fee. These young teachers were then able to cover the cost of making benches for the school, and the brothers created a job for themselves. The number of students attending this school increased weekly. Observing Jonas and Jonathan's commitment and effectiveness, a man in the community offered his newly constructed building as a site for the school.

Determine a Dream: Find a Tree and Get Started
Jonas Atingbui, one of the teachers who, along with his brother Jonathan, found a tree and got started teaching in the community of Nima in Ghana's capital city, Accra.

Jonas, Jonathan, and their students witnessed the power of faith and action. They learned a valuable lesson: just get started—even if the starting point is under a tree—and you can live your dreams.

CHAPTER 1

Yes, You Can Live Your Dream

*"All dreams can come true—if
we have the courage to pursue them."*
—Walt Disney

Our thoughts are our essence. Our dreams are our thoughts for our ideal future, and not necessarily simply a vocation. Our dreams encompass what we love to do. We bring fulfillment to our lives when working toward the realization of our dreams. Realizing our dreams brings about internal peace and makes us a beacon of light for others. Our dreams are the seeds of life. Plant the seeds of a dream and they can grow to become our reality when nurtured with knowledge and action.

How to Live Your Dreams: Find a Tree and Get Started and the corresponding workbook outline the steps readers can take to make their dreams a reality. Life can be a journey of realizing and manifesting your vision and dreams. Giving birth to your vision gives you the drive to learn, achieve, and truly live. Following your dream gives your life meaning, direction, and purpose.

Nurture Your Dreams with Knowledge

I first dreamed of traveling to Africa in the fourth grade after seeing the film *Born Free* and reading about the pyramids in Egypt in third grade. I read about Africa and did a report on the continent. Later, my dream of traveling to Africa came true.

For many, life is a routine of going to uninspiring jobs in order to pay bills. Is our only purpose in life to work to buy things and to pay for what we have already acquired? Is that what life is all about, or do we have more to offer and receive from the world?

We all need material goods, and we all want the best. However, in striving for these possessions, we have lost sight of our true purpose as human beings. Along with material needs, human beings have spiritual needs. We have needs not only in the sense of attending religious ceremonies, but also spiritual needs to create, produce, and manifest our own divine gifts. We all have a need to be recognized and respected for our contributions and talents. If we can discover our purpose and fulfill our personal vision, we can meet our spiritual and psychological needs, attain material wealth, and find the peace and prosperity that all human beings seek.

The failure to live your dream leads to an unfulfilled life. Many have underdeveloped or undiscovered talents and gifts. Failure to access untapped talent leads to unrealized potential. What are the barriers that prohibit so many from having a dream and making it a reality? The failure to pursue your dreams may be caused by a fear of the unknown, fear of financial ruin, or fear of failure.

The failure of so many to pursue their dreams negatively impacts society as well. Society today is filled with frustrated, unfulfilled human beings who have lost the ability to dream. Individuals who suffer from stagnation and the loss of creative power are unable to contribute to society.

The loss of creativity causes individuals to feel as if they are victims at the mercy of others whom they view as "powerful." Individuals and groups who have lost the belief in their own ability to think, create, and manifest are reduced to begging, protesting, petitioning, and resorting to violence. These actions create frustration, destructive behavior, and conflict within society. When individuals are empowered with the realization that they can make their thoughts a reality, they are free from feeling that they are victims. Instead they are on the path to becoming self-empowered builders, producers, and creators. They believe that they can make a difference, not only in their own lives, but also in the lives of those around them.

Create Opportunities through Service
As a result of my work with the Coalition for a Free South Africa at Columbia University, I received a grant from the Ford Foundation to study youth development in Zimbabwe following my graduation from Columbia. *Harare, Zimbabwe, 1985*

By living your dream, you are tapping into your creative power, manifesting your greatness, and sharing with the world your own unique gifts. By living your dream, you, in turn, contribute to building a better world.

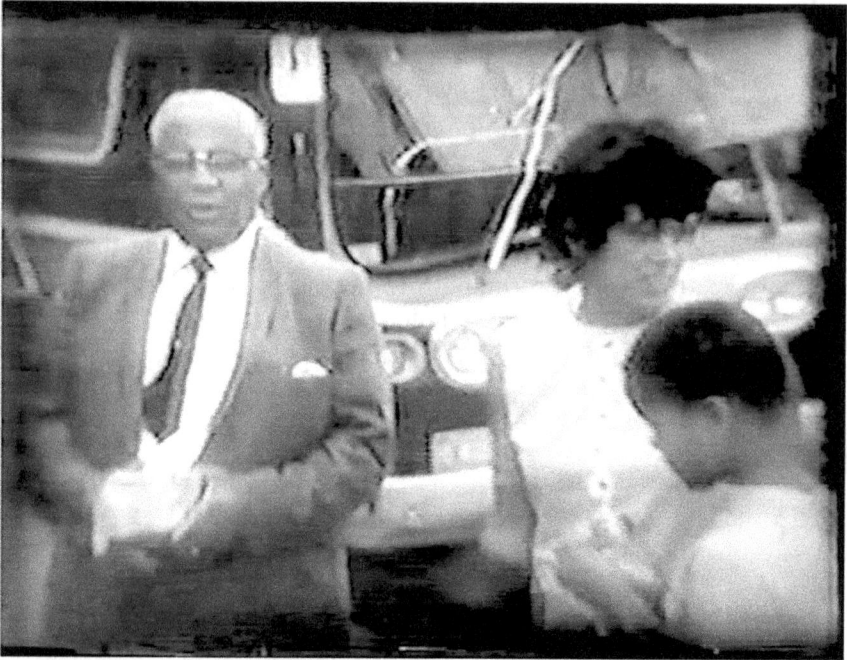

Martin Luther King, Sr.
My mother and me. *Atlanta, Georgia, 1970*

Dreams Are for Now

In second grade I began reading about Martin Luther King, Jr. By the fifth grade I memorized the entire "I Have a Dream" speech. Later I met Dr. King's father, Martin Luther King, Sr., and civil rights icon Rosa Parks.

Rosa Parks
Los Angeles, California, 1987 (Photo by Roland Charles)

When each of us is manifesting our individual dreams, we transform not only our own lives but society as well. Then people will see beyond the superficial and see our true selves. Once we see what each person has to offer, we can increase our harmony and productivity. We all will be giving and sharing our divine gifts and talents. Our individual dreams are interconnected. We can see this interconnection only once we all get in motion living our own dreams.

To help you identify and work toward fulfilling your dreams, use the "Building a Better World Pyramid" in the workbook. It provides an organizational framework for identifying your unique interests, talents, and gifts.

What are you living for?

What is your life's purpose?

THE FIND A TREE PRINCIPLES

1. Identify What You Are Passionate About, Your Interests, Your Talents, and Your Gifts

2. Determine Your Dream: Find a Tree and Get Started

3. Explore Life

4. Nurture Your Dream with Knowledge

5. Empower Yourself

6. Be Willing to March into Hell

7. Build the Trust of Others

8. Embrace Struggle

9. Sometimes You Just Have to Have Faith

10. Create Opportunities through Service

11. Value People

12. Plan, Prioritize, and Manage Your Time

13. Distinguish Yourself with Excellence

14. Understand the Process: From a Seed to a Tree

15. Tap into Your Creative Genius

16. You Will Achieve What You Expect and Try

17. Lead Yourself

18. Start a Business

19. Work in Harmony with Universal Law (There Is No Santa Claus)

CHAPTER 2

Identify What You Are Passionate About, Your Interests, Your Talents, and Your Gifts

*"Have the courage to follow your heart and intuition.
They somehow already know what you truly want to become.
Everything else is secondary."*
—Steve Jobs

"The only way to do great work is to love what you do."
—Steve Jobs

Each of us is born with talents and gifts. There are activities that we love to do and have the ability to do almost effortlessly, activities that we enjoy and would be motivated to do regardless of whether we're paid to do them or not. What gift do you have that you can use to serve others that also gives you satisfaction?

Our talents can be buried deep within us like gold and diamonds. They will have value only if we mine them out of ourselves. First, we have to study our lives to determine what our interests, talents, and gifts are. These abilities can be developed into a project, program, or business. This project, program, or business can be your contribution to the development of your community, nation, and world.

Examine your thoughts, dreams, wishes, and vision. Who are you? What gifts were you blessed with that you could develop and share?

In order to live a fulfilling life, you must discover your gifts and talents, develop them, and give birth to your vision and dream. Only when we are pursuing our dream and working to manifest that vision can we share our inner selves with others. As we each pursue our individual dream and develop our talents and gifts, we will see value in one another and ourselves. It is our personal contribution toward building a better world.

WHO ARE YOU?

From fifth grade until my senior year in high school, I was known to others and myself as "Danny Armstrong: Basketball Star." I had one interest, or rather, obsession: basketball. When I was in eleventh and twelfth grade at Chadwick School, my team rarely lost a game, and I was the star. Our offense was simple: pass the ball to me. After a successful high school career, I found that basketball in college was not like basketball in high school. In college, the offensive plays were numerous, and often I could not remember them in practice. I was no longer the focal point of our offense, but rather of the coach's scorn. Nothing I did during practice was right. I did not play regularly in games, but if I did, I could compete. The coach, Arthur "Buddy" Mahar, was always yelling and cursing, or else he was kicking or reaching to throw something—a crate of sodas, a clipboard, a blackboard—anything. Older players told me that the year before I arrived, he got into a half-court fight with the beloved Princeton coach, Pete Carril. I remember playing Old Dominion University in Virginia and a fan yelled out that our center could not score. Buddy responded with colorful comments about the fan's mother.

In high school, we played before 100 fans on average. My first game in college was against Syracuse University. We were playing the first game in their new Carrier Dome arena. Twenty-six thousand fans showed up for this game. This environment was a lot different from high school.

Practice, Practice, Practice
In college I was often in the gym an hour or two before the team practiced and
would continue to work on my shot after practice was over. Columbia against
Auburn University. *Toledo, Ohio, 1980*

In college I continued to practice obsessively—in the morning before
class, and an hour before and an hour after team practice. I still spent a lot
of time on the bench. Without the status of "star," I felt lost. Gradually,
my attention drifted toward other interests. While one door (or dream)
closing may be frustrating, another door may be opening.

In the fall of my sophomore year at Columbia, I saw a film on apartheid,
the South African government's then-sanctioned policy of racial divi-
sion and oppression, described by the United Nations as "a crime against
humanity." Following this film, the speaker said that Columbia University
had nearly $55 million invested in corporations that operate in South Africa.
The guest spoke of the role divestment could play as an important moral
statement against apartheid if an Ivy League institution revoked its funds.

29

The next day, two other students and I met to plan a forum and to begin organizing the Coalition for a Free South Africa, whose purpose was to educate the Columbia community on apartheid and why the university should divest. The battle was on: the issue was the university's investment policy; the players were three students versus a prestigious university.

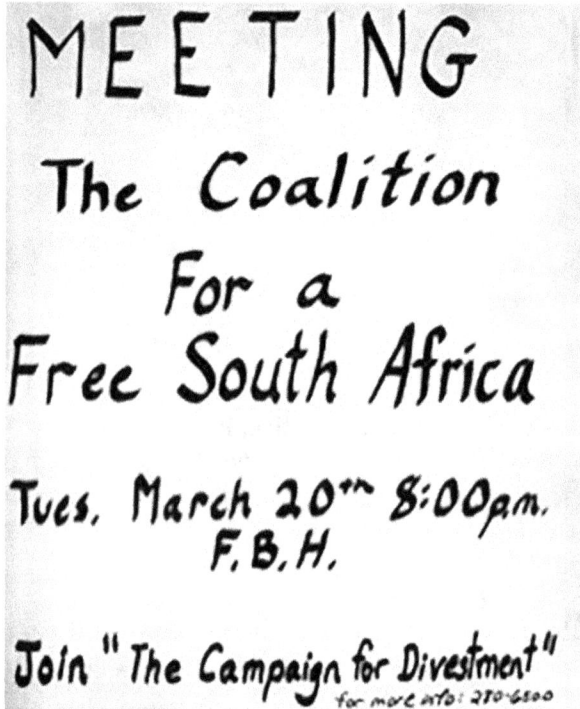

Lead Yourself

I started the Coalition for a Free South Africa after seeing a film about apartheid in South Africa and learning that Columbia University had investments that supported that nation and apartheid. I did not have a computer, email, cell phone, or Facebook, so I handmade fliers that were posted across campus. I shared the phone with roommates who took my calls at all hours of the day and night. Once an exasperated roommate complained to me, "Some guy named Andrew Young called! I told him 'Stop calling!' And I hung up on him!!" I calmly told my frustrated roommate, "That was the mayor of Atlanta."

With limited resources, our fliers were often handwritten announcements of a film, speaker, or discussion session. Although viewed by many as a radical issue, we worked to keep the debate focused on the facts and the humanitarian role the university could play. Authors, ambassadors, members of Congress, and black and white South Africans spoke at our forums and encouraged our efforts. Five months into our campaign we planned our first outdoor rally. I got all the necessary permits to do the rally in the middle of campus where many activities like ours were held. A week before our scheduled rally, a Columbia official realized that our rally was planned on the same day as Dean's Day, the day that guests, donors, and alumni visit the campus. The university had been trying for years to dispel the image of Columbia as a school overrun by student radicals, as Columbia was the site of massive student demonstrations during the 1960s. Administrators were terrified that a divestment rally on Dean's Day would support this image.

A university official informed me that there had been a mistake and that our rally would have to be rescheduled for another day. We recognized that this "conflict" presented us with a great opportunity to present our cause to the university's visiting guests. On behalf of the organization, I insisted that the university abide by our agreement. The student newspaper, the *Columbia Daily Spectator*, got hold of the story. The next day I was on the front page along with the university official who had tried to rescind our agreement. Ultimately, we held our rally. Five people attended in the rain behind the administration building—out of view of the visiting guests.

Initially, I felt alone in moving the campaign forward. Every time I felt like giving up, a stranger would approach and implore me to continue, or someone would offer to make fliers for the organization. I once saw the official in charge of managing the university's investment portfolio quietly purchase a "Columbia Out of South Africa" divestment T-shirt. I was the last person she wanted to see. As our eyes met, she smiled and pleaded with me not to tell that she supported divestment. These moments encouraged me to continue.

As time progressed, the divestment campaign grew to become a major issue on campus. Basketball became less important to me. Instead of getting to practice two hours ahead of time to work on my game, I was dressed and ready to play at 4:29 for a 4:30 p.m. practice. Instead of staying afterwards for an hour to work on my shot, I raced out right after practice to a Coalition meeting or to serve as moderator for a couple hundred people who had come to hear one of our guest speakers. Gradually, my priorities changed from basketball to the South African divestment movement.

We gradually began building a broad base of support. The University Senate, a body of students, faculty, and staff, unanimously supported a resolution for divestment. The Board of Trustees, however, refused to change investment policies. In response, members of the Coalition fasted. We called it "a symbolic sacrifice for others."

In my senior year, the university agreed to freeze investments. A year later, Columbia divested. News of our campaign was reported throughout South Africa. I was told later that our actions had been an inspiration for the people we were working to help. Despite having no resources and only a dream, we got started. Who would have thought that we would be successful? As chairman of the organization, I learned a lot. One lesson was that even as a founder, I had to work as a member of a team. From my colleague, Barbara Ransby, I also learned that when all appears lost, stay with your principles; don't compromise. Truth will eventually triumph.

To survive academically, to play intercollegiate varsity basketball, and to lead the Coalition demanded sacrifice and focus. Effective time management was key. Every minute of my day had to be planned.

"We were the first university with a significant endowment
to resolve to divest its investments in companies
doing business in apartheid South Africa."
—Michael I. Sovern, Former President of Columbia University
An Improbable Life: My 60 Years at Columbia and Other Adventures

---

Columbia University
In the sixth grade I read a book that described how basketball players played basketball on New York City playgrounds until after midnight. I knew then that I had to go to New York City. When I told my guidance counselor that I wanted to go to "the best school in New York City," my counselor told me, "That's Columbia...but you could never get in." Here I am joined by my brother, Don, and my mother on graduation day from Columbia. *New York, New York, 1984*

Chairing the Coalition required that I step out of the comfortable cocoon of being an athlete. I was becoming an activist. My priorities had changed. The action that began my work with the Coalition for a Free South Africa led to many new and exciting adventures.

My self-image expanded beyond basketball. I developed a new vision. I tapped new interests and discovered talents—the ability to organize, to speak, and to lead. This discovery led to the founding of the Coalition for a Free South Africa, Columbia disinvesting over $55 million in companies that supported apartheid, working in Zimbabwe for nine months, and visiting South Africa on a Ford Foundation grant.

After returning from spending the year in Zimbabwe while I was in law and business school at UCLA, I ran into a childhood friend of mine with whom I had played basketball growing up. I asked, "Johnny, what are you doing now?" He replied, "Still trying to make the League (the NBA)." I thought, "Oh, he's still stuck on THAT dream, even at his age." I realized that it was a blessing that my college coach did not play me often. It encouraged me to find other ways to express myself, to explore other facets of who I was, and to develop dreams outside of basketball.

COLUMBIA 👑 SPECTATOR

FOUNDED 1877

MAY 17, 1983   COLUMBIA DAILY SPECTATOR   Page Nineteen

Danny Armstrong:
Off the basketball court, he takes political shots

By LESLIE DREYFOUS

When College junior Danny Armstrong first came to Columbia, he said he wanted to be a starting forward on the basketball team. "It's an example of my going all out. I would get to the gym two hours before practice and stay two hours afterward," he said.

Yet Armstrong's tenacity extends far beyond the basketball court. When he is not reaching for the perfect hook shot, he is working for his political ideas.

"I find that when I set a goal, whether it's basketball or the coalition, I am ready and willing to sacrifice most other things to achieve the objective," he said.

Armstrong was one of three students who founded the Student Coalition to Free South Africa in 1981. "My sister used to tell me about apartheid in South Africa, then my sophomore year, I saw a film about Columbia's investments which in turn supported South Africa," Armstrong recounted. "It hit me that students didn't know what was going on or why Columbia University has investments that in effect support the apartheid system."

The Coalition wants to educate students and parents about Columbia's role in apartheid, he said.

Armstrong recalled the coalition's early days when support was scarce and money even scarcer. "I'd get finished with practice and go to the lockerroom to get my books. The guys would give me a hard time, saying 'Hey Dan, what are you doing? You're a radical.'"

The coalition has since garnered a great deal of support. Teammate "Richie Gordon was one of those guys (in the lockerroom) and now he's a big supporter," noted Armstrong. "That's an example of our success." In addition, Armstrong won the College's Van Am Award in his sophomore year for his work on the Coalition.

The coalition opened students' eyes to the oppressive apartheid regime in South Africa. "We moved into this year and wanted to keep the issue of divestment alive," said Armstrong, "but even more, we wanted to continue education. We started a raffle to pay for a South African student to come here and study, which the

U.N. said is one of the most valuable contributions students can make."

Armstrong described education as "the base to insure a better tomorrow." As the unemployment rate among black teenagers in the United States pushed upwards of 50 per cent, President Reagan continues to rally around a budget which will make essential education even more illusive. "I think the unemployment figures are unacceptable," declared Armstrong. "I want to make sure people aren't victimized."

Education is one of Armstrong's top priorities, his long term goals are equally important. Seeking peace and equal rights and opportunity, Armstrong has completely committed himself to Senator Alan Cranston's bid for the democratic nomination in 1983. "I'm giving up graduating with my class and playing basketball next year so I can spend the time campaigning for Cranston."

"Cranston is the only person that wants to make peace and disarmament a top priority. Even if he doesn't get the nomination, the person that does will have to address the issue," he said.

Pointing to the nuclear threat as the most urgent issue confronting the candidates, he added, "Cranston realizes what can and can't be done, but he's always been a supporter of equal rights for all people."

Clearly energized by the challenges he described, Armstrong's gift of persuasion shines. His conviction is natural and "comes from family influences." Raised outside Los Angeles, Armstrong grew up "with a sense of belief and determination" impressed on him, most particularly by his father who is a lawyer. "I fell any success I have is due to my family. God and they have provided me with a sense of commitment and the ability to direct the energy."

"I am extreme when it comes to fighting for human rights, but I try and balance the short term and the long term."

Armstrong plans to remain "always politically active and involved with things concerned with working for and with people." In the long run Armstrong may run

for public office, but his focus in the short term includes bolstering Cranston's bid at the democratic nomination and "the commitment to raise hell next year if Columbia fails to divest."

His phone will start ringing each morning sometime around 6:00 a.m., but he said he welcomes calls. Immersed in life and the active pursuit of liberty, Armstrong does not regard work as many people do. Commitment and drudgery are far from synonymous for Armstrong, who said he

happily resigns himself to do battle with injustice where human rights are concerned and that his determination is a valuable ally toward victory.

"I want to and should protest for equal rights and opportunity," said Armstrong in a misleading quiet tone. The fire in his eyes betrays him, though. "The issues are vital to all people and I can't consider a commitment of that kind as work. It's a responsibility."

Danny Armstrong

Columbia Daily Spectator, May 17, 1983

34

The "basketball star" label gave me confidence as a young man. However, that label could have become confining if I had not explored other interests. Although basketball served its purpose in my life, I was fortunate to have moved on with other dreams.

Explore your full range of interests. Stereotypes and established self-images are like walls that may be comfortable, but can also be confining. Sometimes we must step outside our self-image to discover and extract the full spectrum of who we are and the talents that lie within.

A sport is a microcosm of life. The characteristics needed to succeed mirror the qualities required to live your dream. These characteristics include self-confidence when facing a challenge, discipline, teamwork, sacrifice, and hard work. Unfortunately, many young athletes who dream of playing in college or professionally never tap into talents outside of those required to perform their sport. Consequently, some athletes drift through school and life with no sense of purpose other than playing their sport.

What untapped talents and interests do you have?

Make a list of twenty interests, talents, and gifts that you have.

You are more than a basketball player, football player, a mom, or however you have labeled yourself.

Who are you?

You are more than what you think.

CHAPTER 3

Determine Your Dream: Find a Tree and Get Started

"Nothing happens unless first a dream."
—Carl Sandburg

"Winning starts with beginning."
—Robert H. Schuller

In order to live your dream, you must first have a dream. The dream is the seed.

From your list of twenty interests, talents and gifts, create groupings of talents and interests that complement each other. What activity would utilize these talents and interests? Stretch your mind. Allow yourself to focus on what you want, not the reasons it will not work or the obstacles you will face. Dream.

FINDING YOUR TREE

What can you do today to work toward your dream? Reduce your dream to its simplest component. The starting point for most dreams is getting information about your dream. Begin by reading. Next, talk to people who have done what you dream of doing or may have knowledge of your area of interest. Find out how they did it and seek their advice to create your own road map. Determine the process you will have to undertake to gain understanding, proficiency, and the ability to launch your dream. Focus on what you have at your disposal today, and begin there. Plan for how you will proceed once you have more resources, but for now, start where you are. For example, if you dream of one day opening a restaurant of your own, but do not have the resources to do that, start by making food in your own kitchen and catering special events held by friends and family members. Your kitchen will be your tree.

Your dream can only begin once you take action.
Do something today.
It all begins with a dream.

They Found Their Tree
No Tree? Use the Stairs
The Otha Johnson III Story

At Compton High School, I was not given a classroom to teach the Find A Tree program. We met in the cafeteria. Then one day a student ran across the cafeteria tables, and the director of food services kicked us out of the cafeteria. After we were asked not to meet in the gym, our only alternative was to meet behind the cafeteria on six cement steps. From our "classroom" on the stairs, students shared their interests and dreams. Several students wanted to be in the music business. When I asked them a basic question about the music industry, they could not answer. I asked them, "How are you going to be successful if you do not know anything about the industry?" So students, under the leadership of one senior, Otha Johnson, organized a music business study group to read about the music business and share their findings with each other. Next, the students organized a music business seminar, in which industry executives came to the school and held workshops that focused on career opportunities other than performing. Participating students then had an opportunity to meet with music executives in their offices. Students were given the opportunity to apply for an internship with the Y.E.S. to Jobs program, a summer jobs program in the entertainment industry for students. Otha applied to the Y.E.S. to Jobs program and was employed by Capitol Records, a major record label. Otha called me one day during the summer to tell me that that afternoon he had a one-on-one meeting with the president of Capitol. I asked him if he knew how many musicians and agents in the world would love to have a face-to-face meeting with the president of Capitol Records. I reminded Otha that he had gone from our class on the stairs behind the cafeteria by the dumpsters to a meeting with the president of Capitol. At the end of the summer, Otha was selected by the Y.E.S. to Jobs program as one of the top students in the program based on employer comments.

The July 2002 edition of *Source Magazine*, a national music industry publication, featured a story about Otha.

Otha recalled his experience in the Find A Tree program in a recent interview:

"The Find A Tree program gave me the insight needed to take action. The Find A Tree book is what I call the 'Bible of Business.' No matter what obstacle or situation is present, the Find A Tree program can help you understand that you still have an opportunity. At Compton High School we moved around a lot and never had a standard classroom, but we still had class. We were kicked out of the cafeteria and banned from the P.E. area until we found ourselves on the steps outside of the cafeteria. But we were still a class and made things happen for ourselves despite our obstacles. Some of Mr. Armstrong's students were gang members and criminals, but the message was still the same: do not let your current obstacles or conditions stop you from pursuing your dream. Any book that can help a person turn his life around, help him change his condition, and at the same time teach business principles, is definitely the 'Bible of Business.' Never give up. Follow your dreams. I am a living witness."

CHAPTER 4

Explore Life

"It's a helluva start, being able to recognize what makes you happy."
—Lucille Ball

Become proactive regarding your career and life. Start today exploring the possibilities. Through exploration, you may only find what you do not want, but in time you will find what is right for you.

I asked a student who was heading off to Harvard University what she was going to study in college. She said, "I don't know." I asked, "Well, why are you going to college?" This highly motivated honors student responded to my question with the same bewildered reply, "I don't know."

I soon found out that this Ivy League–bound student was not an exception. Many students attend school and graduate with no sense of purpose or understanding why they are there. Explore life by doing a self-inventory to determine why and what you want to pursue during your academic career and following graduation.

In high school I wanted to be a journalist. For my senior project I worked at the local NBC news affiliate. At NBC I would spend the day with the reporters in the field and watch them produce their stories in the afternoon for the evening broadcast. I got to see firsthand what I envisioned that I wanted to do one day. One sports reporter, who I got to meet at the station, became a nationally known anchor, Bryant Gumbel. This experience fed my interest in journalism.

A week after my high school graduation, I left California for Columbia University in New York City. I had made arrangements with the basketball coach at Columbia, and he promised a summer job and the opportunity to play in a summer league. I had always heard that college coaches arranged easy and well-paying jobs for their players. I assumed that I would be working on Wall Street, at the *New York Times*, at the United Nations, or at ABC Sports with Columbia alumni.

As my flight descended on New York's JFK airport, I recall the flight attendant giving the local weather, landing logistics, and then she concluded by saying, "Welcome to the real world." "What did she mean?" I wondered. "Isn't L.A. 'the real world?'"

I soon realized what the flight attendant meant. Once I arrived in New York, the Columbia coach told me that I would be working on Broadway. I imagined the excitement of working in theater.

Monday morning I reported to the job the Columbia coach had arranged for me. I quickly realized I would not be working in the theater district. My job was to dig weeds on Broadway Avenue. I was seventeen years old. It was my first time away from home, and I was miserable. This was the "real world."

Explore Life

Eager to leave home, I moved to New York City during the summer before my freshman year at Columbia University. The basketball coach promised me a job. My job was to dig weeds on Broadway Avenue. After less than a month I got fired for not digging fast enough. My father responded to my dismissal by telling me, "Never call home again and never ask for any more money. Goodbye."

After about three days on the job, I called my mother from a pay phone on Broadway during my morning break and just started crying. My older brother sent me a note saying that he always knew that I would make it to "Broadway." He included a 10% off discount coupon from a hardware store for a weed eater tool. I did not find any humor in his letter. After a few weeks, I got fired for not digging fast enough. Relieved that my "real world" experience was over, I called my father to report that I had been fired and was ready to return home for the rest of the summer.

Instead of instructing me to make travel plans, my father said, "Son, do not call here ever again, and do not ask for any more money. Goodbye." He then hung up the phone. My father was not the joking type. I knew he was serious. Stunned, I immediately envisioned myself as homeless pushing a shopping cart.

I had already paid my rent for the dorm room for the summer. I just had to stretch my savings to buy food. I learned that every afternoon on campus in Earl Hall, cookies and tea were served while violin music played. I made a point of being there every day and ate as many free cookies as I could.

By mid-summer, I began to count the days before I would go home the following spring—294…293…292…291…

With my time now free, I volunteered to help the Democratic Party organize its national convention. My contribution was to move chairs. I hoped that if I showed up every day wearing a tie, some new assignment would come. Soon after, my chair-moving stint led to working for the press information office. Once the convention began, I found myself free to roam the floor of the convention. As a future student of political science, I was in heaven.

Two images made me reconsider my journalism career choice. The first one was a mature, balding man seated on the floor of a corridor of Madison Square Garden with a manual typewriter between his spread legs. He was frantically typing his story to meet his impending deadline. I could not picture myself doing that at his stage of life. The second image was a wave of reporters chasing after a politician who did not want to talk to them. I could not see myself chasing after someone who did not want to talk to me. These two experiences shifted my career aspirations.

I had selected a path, explored it, and determined it was not for me. The path you choose may be one you change, but it is better to explore and determine what you want to do instead of waiting to see what falls your way. Explore your interests.

After I investigated a career in journalism, my interest shifted to politics, so I majored in political science at Columbia.

In my junior year, two friends, Rik Leeds and Mark Simon, invited me to hear United States Senator Alan Cranston of California speak on campus. Afterwards Rik, Mark, and I interviewed Senator Cranston for our student newspaper. Mark and Rik respectfully grilled the Senator with a barrage of policy and legislative questions. I was amazed at their knowledge. Senator Cranston was too. Afterwards, I asked Mark and Rik how they knew so much about politics. They said they read the *New York Times* from front to back—every day. The next day, I bought a subscription to the *Times* and began reading too—every day.

Senator Cranston, who was laying the foundation to run for the presidency of the United States, invited Mark, Rik, and me to meet with him in a few weeks in Washington, D.C. to discuss the campaign. We arrived in Washington the day before our meeting. A staff member invited us to watch the evening's Senate proceedings in the visitors' gallery. Mark and Rik were determined to let Senator Cranston, who spotted us in the gallery, know that we were serious, so we decided to stay until the Senate recessed for the evening. The Senate adjourned at 3:00 a.m., just five hours before our meeting with the Senator and his chief of staff. By the time we left the Senate it was almost 4:00 a.m., and the place we were staying was at least an hour away. We decided to share a bench outside of the Capitol and slept there for a couple of hours.

The birds awakened us at daybreak. Looking disheveled, we scrambled into a Capitol restroom to wash our faces, brush our teeth, and prepare to meet with the Majority Whip of the United States Senate and presidential candidate to-be, Alan Cranston, the senior Senator from California.

I do not remember much of the meeting, other than the fact that Mark, Rik, and I kept dozing off. Finally, as the meeting wound down, sitting across from Cranston, the three us went to sleep simultaneously as the Senator spoke to us about organizing college students for his presidential campaign.

When a staff member cleared his throat, we awoke sheepishly. We had to admit that we did not sleep the night before, other than resting on a bench outside the Capitol. Senator Cranston thought it was funny and then hosted us in the Senators' private dining room. At lunch Rik and Mark giddily chatted as they recognized the Senators who came for lunch. I only recognized Bill Bradley from New Jersey because he had played professional basketball with the New York Knicks.

Following our meeting, we were offered opportunities to work full time on the Cranston campaign. Knowing Senator Cranston as well as key members of his campaign staff personally, I accepted the campaign manager's offer. This acceptance meant I would have to take a year off from school.

Working in the campaign's Washington, D.C. headquarters the summer before my senior year, I got to see a presidential campaign up close. This work meant lots of speeches (usually the same one). Staff members would stand in back of an auditorium and often recite the candidate's stump speech in unison with him as he spoke on stage. We distributed literature, shook hands, and tried to convince people to support Senator Cranston.

In late June of that summer, while riding a Washington bus to work, I briefly met a lady and launched into my "Vote for Cranston" patter. I promised to send her literature. I did not. Months later while walking down the street, this same lady stopped and said in a voice that only a mother could deliver, "You did not send me that information!" Confused, I quickly remembered, "You're the lady on the bus!" I walked a few blocks with her to her office and within an hour, she convinced me to leave the campaign and return to school. Senator Cranston's campaign did not last long, and going back to school proved to be a wise decision. The lady on the bus, Ms. Johnnie Griffin, attended my college graduation and has remained a family friend.

People come into your life when you need them to.

The following summer, I again found myself working for the Democratic Party, organizing for its national convention in San Francisco. I worked for Amelia Parker, then director of the Office of Black Affairs for the Democrats. She taught me that the workday does not end at 5 p.m. when phones stop ringing, but only begins. Parker also taught me to go beyond others' expectations. During that time, I also had the opportunity to work as an assistant to the late Ron Brown, who later became Secretary of Commerce for former President Clinton.

Presidential candidate, **the Reverend Jesse Jackson, Sr.,** at the 1984 Democratic National Convention. *San Francisco, California, 1984*

From moving chairs to being an assistant to Ms. Parker, Senator Cranston, and Secretary Brown, I could not have imagined a better position to view the world of politics. The lesson I learned was not only to get started, but also to remember that my beginning point is not necessarily my ending point. Ironically, these exciting experiences in politics showed me that I did not want to pursue a career in politics. By being proactive, however, I got to see the inner workings of politics firsthand before making that choice.

No path of action is a mistake. You will learn invaluable lessons along the way, even if the ultimate lesson is that the particular path you're on is not the one you want to pursue. Failing to take any action is the only mistake.

STUDENTS: START NOW!

While a student in UCLA's Masters in Business Administration program, a team of students was assigned to select a corporation and interview an executive to discuss his or her decision-making procedures and policies. Since we had the opportunity to select any company and any official, and since my classmates and I were all sports enthusiasts, we chose the Los Angeles Lakers basketball team and the company president, former NBA great, Jerry West. Mr. West was my boyhood idol, so the thought of meeting him was exciting. A member of our team called the Lakers and told the secretary that we were UCLA students doing research and wanted to meet with Mr. West about his management philosophy and decision-making procedures. Mr. West called back and made an appointment to meet with us.

Mr. West spent about two hours discussing the Lakers, his philosophy on selecting and trading players, and maintaining team chemistry. My four classmates were less knowledgeable about basketball than I, so I had what was almost a one-on-one talk with West.

Students Start Now!

Former NBA great and then Los Angeles Lakers' president, **Jerry West**, meets with fellow UCLA students and me to discuss his management of the Lakers. *Inglewood, California, 1993*

If we had called and said we were avid Laker fans and wanted to talk basketball with Jerry West, we would not have gotten past the ticket office. The title "student" opens doors. Use this key to gain access to people who would otherwise be unreachable.

For another project while at UCLA, we had to interview an executive about his or her life story. I chose a CEO who seemed never to have time to meet with me. After more than a month of being put off by his secretary, I asked if I could come down and wait until he had a free minute. Clearly, this was going to be a battle of wills. I was prepared to stay as long as I had to. I brought my books and food, and I set up shop in the company's lobby. I waited for five and a half hours. As the CEO was leaving the office for the day, he saw me still waiting. He realized that I refused to leave and was determined to interview him. He took me to dinner, and we have remained in contact ever since. While many may be willing, executives' busy schedules may require that you be patient and persistent.

Few know instinctively what they want to do with their lives. Like climbing a mountain trail, most must explore various options, as some trails may not lead to the intended destination. To reach our dream we have to be prepared to explore many paths and climb many mountains until we find the one that leads to our dream.

CHAPTER 5

Nurture Your Dream with Knowledge

"Without knowledge, action is useless and knowledge
without action is futile."
—Abu Bakr

KNOWLEDGE + ACTION = YOUR DREAM

Without a vision to work toward, human beings become lifeless. For example, many students are bored in school. Often they see no connection between life and sitting in a classroom. If they were encouraged to identify and develop a dream, and to use school as a means to achieve their vision, then many would find education a useful and relevant experience.

Classrooms have to be more than a place to prepare students for a job that pays them money so they can buy nice things. This idea is especially true today since illegal activities can provide much more money than the typical job. Without a vision and the motivation that comes from living for its achievement, students pursue destructive and unproductive activities.

This condition is living death. By working with students toward the realization of their dreams, today's classrooms can be transformed from chaos to creative centers of learning and discovery.

Education comes from the Latin root "educere," which means "to bring out," "draw out," and "to lead." Through education, students should learn how to bring out, draw out, and develop their natural talents. In addition to gaining academic proficiency, students should learn and develop the ability to transform their thoughts into reality. After graduating, students can then turn their gifts or talents into a business to lead a company of their own. The purpose of education would be to equip and empower students to live their dream.

Following my undergraduate education at Columbia University, in New York City, I received a Ford Foundation grant to study youth development in Zimbabwe. I studied government programs and schools in that African nation. While I was visiting one school, a teacher complained to me that the students arrived at school an hour early and waited until classrooms opened, and that administrators had to force them to leave at the end of day. At one point during my visit, the teacher told the class to keep reading while she took me on a tour of the campus. When we returned one hour later, every student was still reading. No student had moved other than to turn the page of his or her book. Knowing what I would have done myself as a young student in the absence of a teacher, I looked at the teacher in amazement. I said, "Ma'am, do you know that in Los Angeles...someone could have been dead by now?"

Zimbabwean Classroom

Teachers complained that students arrived at school an hour early and wanted to continue to learn at the end of the school day. A teacher and I left her classroom for one hour to tour the campus. While we were gone, the unsupervised students continued to read. I advised the teacher that in many classrooms in Los Angeles, things would be a little different after an hour of absence.

From my study, I realized that the students in Zimbabwe perceived a direct connection between what they want to do—their dream—and being in the classroom. They felt empowered with the knowledge that they would have to run their nation one day, and school was the means by which they could realize their dream.

In the fall of 2000, the Find A Tree program was contracted at Compton High School in California. The school district had been taken over by the state because of financial mismanagement and years of poor test scores. Posted in front of the school was a grade for cleanliness: "F." Although I grew up in Compton, my parents sent me primarily to private schools outside of the district, so this was the first time I spent time in a Compton school since first grade. The school seemed to be in a constant state of chaos. Students walked the campus during class time. Assistant principals shouted and yelled instructions to students about a cap, a fight, or graffiti on school walls. Students complained about locked bathrooms (a locked bathroom could not get dirty, reasoned the administration). Security guards patrolled the campus. For many teachers, it was an accomplishment just to get through the day without an incident. An assistant principal complained that she once called in a student's parents because the student was still active in his gang. Not long into the student-parent conference, this administrator helplessly realized that the parents were still involved in gangs themselves. Despite this environment, I met many concerned and dedicated teachers, administrators, and students who seemed enthusiastic about pursing their dreams through the Find A Tree program. I spent my first weeks making presentations to the students in English classes. One student had the dream of becoming a screenwriter, but did not know how school and English class in particular connected to her dream. There was a large gulf between curriculum and the students' aspirations. Once the connection is made between learning and the students' goals, students have a greater desire to read and learn.

After being at Compton for a month, the administration identified fifty ninth graders who needed special attention and direction to stay focused and out of trouble. Most of the students selected for the Find A Tree program had long track records of missing school, ditching classes, or being suspended. I called the group "The Leaders." Compton had many fine students, but The Leaders were determined to create havoc wherever they went. I began with these students on the basketball court. I figured if they knew we were going to play ball, they were more likely to show up for school and my class. Once I garnered a degree of discipline, we moved toward a more traditional class setting. One student in the Find A Tree class was Jeffrey McLeod. Jeffery had a way of challenging teachers, his mother, and his peers with his behavior. At one point, after Jeffrey had repeatedly interrupted our class, the students unanimously voted Jeffrey out of the Find A Tree class. Reason: he was too disruptive. For this class to deem one of its own as "too disruptive," one could only imagine what type of behavior that required. After Jeffrey protested, they reluctantly rescinded their vote. Jeffrey, despite all of his antics, had a passionate interest in architecture. One day Jeffrey was preparing to have a fight with another student during class, and he refused to listen to me or to the security guard. I dragged him away from the fight and declared with frank honesty, "Jeffrey, one day, you are either going to be a great architect, or you are going to jail!"

When I got Jeffrey books on architecture, he read them and asked for more. When I asked him if he wanted to wake up early on a Saturday and do construction work with the non-profit group Habitat for Humanity, an organization that builds low-cost housing, Jeffrey was an eager volunteer. Unfortunately, he could not participate, as he did not meet their minimum age requirement. I took Jeffrey and two other students to a breakfast meeting at the home of an architect to gain insight on how one becomes an architect. At breakfast Jeffrey asked questions, participated in the discussion, and was interested in what the architects shared. I quietly told one, "If you only knew how Jeffrey often behaves, you would not recognize him today." Any time I talked to Jeffrey about what he had to do to become an architect following that meeting, he was interested. Acknowledging his propensity to be a distraction and unfocused, Jeffrey, referring to architecture, told me, "Now *that* I am serious about." Jeffery was even helpful and interested in finding out if he could take an architectural course at the local community college. Although it was hard to get him to go to class at Compton High School, he was now looking to take an additional course.

To engage Jeffrey in school there had to be a direct connection between his class work and becoming an architect. Without this connection, he was lost, disinterested, a distraction to all around him. By bridging the gap, he became a focused and eager student.

To transform classrooms from chaos to creative centers of learning, students must be motivated to learn. This motivation must come from making education relevant by directly linking students' dreams to the curriculum taught. First, that dream must be identified. Then students must understand the connection of each subject to their dreams and the idea that mastering the subject will better enable them to live their dream.

Dreams require knowledge and action to make them a reality. The first step is to read about your dream and area of interest. Connect term papers and research projects to your dream. Meet and interview people doing what you dream of doing. Work as an intern with companies in the area of your interest.

CHAPTER 6

Empower Yourself

*"If you wait until all conditions are perfect before you act,
you'll never act."*

—Anonymous

Decide today to dream. Take action to make your dream your reality. Depending on others to empower you or to bring you what you need to realize your dream will leave you with just hopes and wishes. Blaming others for your plight will not advance your dream. Take responsibility for your dream by not giving someone else the power to determine your future. Empower yourself by accepting the responsibility for making your life what you want it to be. Empowerment begins with creating a vision of what you want and taking action to make your vision a reality.

Have you empowered someone else to decide your future?

JUDGMENTS

Pursuing your dream may put you on a unique path. Others may not understand your chosen path or agree with it. Empowering yourself is having the faith that you must proceed and accept the consequences—whether that means success or failure—and accept the criticism of others. Listen to those around you, but ultimately, you must decide how you will live your life and what you want from your life. Those judging you must live theirs. When you think of those casting disparaging judgments, would you consider trading the realization of your dream for the reality that they recommend you pursue? If not, continue to find your tree and nurture your dream. Associate yourself with positive people who are supportive and can offer helpful advice and counsel.

What people or circumstances are you permitting to block your progress toward the realization of your dream?

Look to no one else to approve or grant you permission. You are empowered once you decide to dream. Visualize your goal or objective. Then find your tree and get started.

CHAPTER 7

Be Willing to March into Hell

"Every winner has scars."
—*Herbert N. Casson*

"The ultimate measure of a man is not where he stands during times of comfort and convenience, but where he stands during times of challenge and controversy."
—*Martin Luther King, Jr.*

When you pursue your dreams, you could be marching right into hell.

Enduring battles, pain, and turmoil can follow when you decide to realize your dream. However, this test of fire prepares you to reach not only your dream, but your human potential as well.

I experienced the trials of pursuing a dream as a graduate student at UCLA when I organized an international conference of business students, executives, and government officials. My dream evolved from my experiences in Zimbabwe.

While in Zimbabwe, the world watched Ethiopians endure famine. Entertainers sang, "We Are the World." Having seen industry and development in Zimbabwe, I knew that if current and future businesspeople could come together to develop trade, tragedies such as those seen in Ethiopia would not have to take place.

Three years later, while enrolled in the law and business schools at UCLA, my friend Edward Lawson and I discussed bringing students and businesspeople together in an organization that would address the issues and concerns of establishing trade with Africa. After that conversation, I decided to form the International Black Masters of Business Administration Student Association (I*B*MBASA). Six months after the organization was formed, we organized the International Black MBA Student Conference, which was held on the UCLA campus December 27–31, 1988.

The conference brought together students from across the United States, Canada, the Caribbean, and Africa to discuss economic development. Guest speakers included government officials, sports figures, and businesspeople from around the world.

Knockout

Former heavyweight champion **Mike Tyson** attended the sports management workshop at the International Black MBA Student Association Conference, which I organized as a graduate student at UCLA. *Los Angeles, California, December 28, 1988* (Photo by Roland Charles)

Although we achieved our dream, both the organization and I personally finished the conference in tremendous debt. The fallout from the conference, in addition to our debt, was humiliation, a formal resolution of condemnation from my peers, and attempts by UCLA administrators to deny me my degrees. The lessons of I*B*MBASA were immense. Friends who had supported the conference and my efforts lost money. Although the vast majority of the debt was incurred without my knowledge or approval, as chairman of the organization I had to take responsibility. Yet, this failure was a blessing. In this failure, I learned lifelong lessons that no textbook could have taught me.

LESSONS OF I*B*MBASA

1. Face Your Creditors

It is a lot easier to avoid creditors than to face their verbal slugs. I did not always face mine. I learned that it is often better to listen to them express their right to payment, their hardship as a result of the debt, and what they are prepared to do to get their money. When their tirade is over, share with them your appreciation of their patience and your plan of action to pay the debt. Confirm your plan to them in writing as a follow-up. Creditors only get angrier and more determined when you avoid them. When I communicated with them, some actually became cooperative.

2. Ask Tough Questions

Sometimes we have to ask difficult questions of people, especially when we are in a position of authority. Doing what is right is more important than remaining friends. Lots of people will get angry with you, but you still have to ask the questions and take appropriate action.

3. "Three Flag Rule"

Watch people. Their character will be revealed through their actions—good and bad. I was blind to indications that a staff member was operating in a less than appropriate manner. From that experience,

I learned to keep my eyes open. If I observe an act that suggests poor character and integrity, I raise a mental red flag, provided that the offense is minor. At that point, I am alert to be watchful for flag number two. If another act occurs, I know a third red flag is waiting to be exposed. After the third red flag, it is best to cease all involvement with that person or risk being burned. Use your judgment on how severe an act must be to raise a flag.

4. Keep Documentation

"He with the most documentation wins." —Yolanda M. Parker

Keep records. You never know when you will have to recreate a trail of events. In business, get commitments in writing, even from friends.

5. When You Succeed, It's Because of the Team; When You Fail, You Are Responsible

Accept the responsibility of leadership. Do not run from it. You will ultimately grow and benefit from accepting responsibility when under fire.

6. There Is a Thin Line Between Success and Failure

Never get too down when you fail or too proud when you succeed; you may have been very close to being on the other side. It took me several years to recover from the financial and emotional trauma of this experience. Despite the difficulties, I would have done the conference again, as this was my dream. Learning the lessons of I*B*MBASA was hell, but it prepared me for future endeavors.

CHAPTER 8

Build the Trust of Others

"The one who follows the crowd will usually get no further than the crowd. The one who walks alone, is likely to find himself in places no one has ever been."

—*Albert Einstein*

Throughout the process of actualizing your dream, you will need the support of others who trust you. You may need a recommendation, a referral, or financial support. Building the trust and support of others will, at some point, become critical in moving your dream forward.

In September 1999, I began the Find A Tree course at the Fred C. Nelles Youth Correctional Facility, a jail for juvenile offenders in Whittier, California. During the first month of the curriculum, I worked with youth sixteen to nineteen years old on the importance of one's character in realizing their dreams. The young men, who were incarcerated for crimes ranging from drug use to murder, listened respectfully for the first week or two to their new instructor. By the third week I heard through the staff that they were getting tired of hearing about character. By the fourth week they were bold enough to let me know that they had signed up for the Find A Tree course to figure out how to open a business and make "big money." Recognizing their dissatisfaction, I said, "Fine. We'll talk about building a business." Now they were excited. They took out their notebooks for the first time in weeks and wrote feverishly as I talked about the elements of a business plan. Then I got to the area of financing a business. I shared that many entrepreneurs go to banks and get loans. The students gleamed with excitement as they imagined themselves leaving jail, entering a bank, and walking out with millions of dollars—as a "loan." I quoted from a bank newsletter title "The 5 C's of Credit." I explained to the students what the bank said they look for in making loans. The article stated that "collateral," "conditions," and "capital and capacity" were important factors when considering a loan application. The students could not write fast enough to soak in this information and prepare to get a loan upon their release. I concluded that evening's lesson by sharing with them what the article said was the bank's most important factor when considering a loan applicant: "character." As I shared this final and most important criterion, pencils dropped in disbelief. They said they got my point. Character first.

Find A Tree students, along with counselor Patrick Czarny, from the Fred C. Nelles Youth Correctional Facility. *Whittier, California, 2000*

Character is demonstrated in the smallest things that we do. Keeping our word, even for simple things. How often do we say, "Oh, I'll call you tomorrow," and never do? When handling someone else's money, do we return all the change and account for all monies even if it's only a few dollars or a few cents? This is character. Being on time and returning items borrowed reflects our character. Accepting responsibility and not blaming others reflects our character. These little actions build the trust of others, so that when you need their help, they know that they can trust and depend on you.

Transformation

Darwin Ramirez spent a year in a cell by himself for 23 hours a day before joining the Find A Tree class. He left jail and worked for BMG Entertainment in Beverly Hills, California. His supervisor said he was one of the best young employees they had ever had.

While operating my own carpet cleaning business, I had to determine whom to hire. I first reasoned that it would be better to hire someone who has a family and dependents, as he would be reliable given his responsibilities. This formula proved to be faulty. Next, I decided to hire someone young and eager to make money, but he also proved to be unreliable. Finally, I decided to take prospective employees to the basketball court. I did not care how good they were at dribbling or shooting; my goal was to get them tired and then see how they responded on the court when tired. Did they slack off or did they continue to play hard? If they played hard, regardless of the number of shots they missed, I offered them a job. If they quit once they got tired, they were not offered a position. This formula proved to be reliable. People's character became evident once they were faced with fatigue and the challenge of playing tired. One's character is consistent whether working on a project, job, or playing sports.

When faced with a challenge, examine your response. Develop character that people can trust. This practice will benefit you when you need help.

CHAPTER 9

Embrace Struggle

"What makes life mean something is purpose...the goal...the battle...the struggle...even if you don't win."
—Richard Nixon

"The greatness comes not when things go always good for you, but the greatness comes and you are really tested, when you take some knocks, some disappointments, when sadness comes, because only if you have been in the deepest valley can you ever know how magnificent it is to be on the highest mountain."
—Richard Nixon

"It's fine to celebrate success, but it is more important to heed the lessons of failure."
—Bill Gates

Struggle builds our character. Struggle builds our foundation. Struggle increases our knowledge and understanding. The opportunity to struggle is a blessing.

The process may be painful or demand sacrifice and focus, but this preparation is necessary. The struggle is our education. The curriculum of struggle will make us a master. A master is an expert, a leader, a teacher, and a supreme being.

Struggle is the road to mastery. Mastery will produce excellence. Excellence will enable us to create a job for ourselves and to live our dream. To get to this level, we often have to go through the challenge of failure. Failure, like struggle, can be a blessing if we understand and learn from it. Struggle can bring out your creative genius, which is particularly needed when your resources appear limited.

I could not find a summer job after my first year of college. I assumed that as an Ivy League student, jobs would be easy to find. After numerous rejections, I went to the local McDonald's and applied. They rejected me because I would be returning to school in three months, and, therefore, not worth training.

Crises can be a danger or an opportunity. The danger was facing my parents if I did not find a job. The opportunity came when I decided to become an entrepreneur. With a $15 investment, I started my own business: Danny's Carpet Cleaning Service.

I borrowed my mother's vacuum and scrub brushes. My first fliers were handwritten. I sent them to my neighbors, family, and friends. Despite soaking a few carpets in the beginning, I learned and always tried to do a good job. The business grew, and I hired an assistant.

WHEN WAS THE LAST TIME YOUR CARPETS WERE STEAM CLEANED ?
3 years... 4 years ... can't remember ?

Dannys Carpet Cleaning Service

will:
1. thoroughly vacuum
2. move most furniture
3. pre-clean carpet with special attention to spots and walkways
4. steam clean carpet
5. deodorize
6. apply carpet protector (additional charge)

Quality at a Low Price

Call today... have "new" carpets tomorrow !

Danny Armstrong
(213) 636-6734

... since 1981

Use Your Talents to Create a Job for Yourself

I grew up cleaning my dad's office so I knew how to clean. Following my first year at Columbia, I was unable to find a summer job. I borrowed my mother's vacuum and buckets, and with a $15 investment to rent a carpet cleaning machine, I launched "Danny's Carpet Cleaning Service."

The next summer I felt I needed a "real" job, but when I learned what companies pay, I knew I could make more money cleaning carpets. So I continued the business and hired more staff. The staff did the cleaning; I focused on marketing.

Having your own business means if you do not get customers, you do not eat. I could not afford expensive advertising, so I would go door to door to sell our services. All door-to-door selling is tough. I was asking residents to permit me, a six-foot-five-inch stranger, to walk through their home. From the privacy of their bedrooms to an untidy family room, I could see all of their dirt. Even though I knew that many needed our services, the fear of a stranger's seeing their unkempt home prevented many sales. However, I could not use excuses to explain a lack of business. My staff and I had to eat. A solution had to be found.

Struggle can produce answers that you may not otherwise realize.

The company's name was changed to the Dirt Patrol. No longer just carpet cleaners, we became "Grime Fighters," out to "arrest" dirt lurking in carpets, drapes, and upholstery. We declared "war against grime." I became the self-proclaimed "Chief Grime Fighter of Los Angeles," out to reform "dirtaholics" who were "leading a life of grime." Our vehicles were painted like police cars. We had a "Neighborhood Grime Watch" program, where neighbors would call me on the "Dirt Hotline" (299-DIRT) to report neighbors who were "griminals"—those leading a "life of grime" and who refused to "come clean." I would then visit the "grime scene," and advise residents of their "grime rights" (that their home had a right to remain spotless; any dirt found could and would be removed). I was hard against grime. I threatened to put all griminals on "dirt row," unless they cleaned up their act. Like the Betty Ford Clinic, we had the "Dirty Floor Clinic," a twelve-step program for dirtaholics. Many pleaded "griminal insanity." These were people who were in denial, refusing to admit the problem and blaming someone else for their filthy condition.

A Totally New Concept In CARPET CLEANING
"SHAMPOO & STEAM CLEAN AT NO EXTRA COST!"

METICULOUS CLEANING SINCE 1981
— "WE TREAT EACH JOB LIKE OUR OWN HOME" —

"GRIME FIGHTERS"

We'll arrest the dirt and grime in your
carpets • upholstery • drapes
SOIL EXTRACTION • WATER DAMAGE
SPOT REMOVAL • HAND SCRUBBING
PET ODOR PROBLEMS • QUICK DRYING • MOST FURNITURE MOVED

D·P

Dirt Patrol
cleaning services

24-HOUR
DIRT HOTLINE

299-DIRT

FREE
QUOTES

Fighting Grime, Not Crime

My company grew and I changed the company name to the "Dirt Patrol."

Because of our use of humor, homeowners welcomed us into their dirty homes to see their filthy carpets and dusty drapes. I pledged that their mess was our dirty secret. Once the potential customer started laughing, she or he would often get on the phone to tell friends about the Dirt Patrol and our efforts to take a "bite out of grime." Radio stations even let me come on the air for free to tell "dirt jokes" and promote the campaign against grime. We could never have afforded to pay for all this advertising. Our client list grew from cleaning friends' and neighbors' houses to cleaning hotels, a downtown skyscraper, military bases, and a prestigious country club.

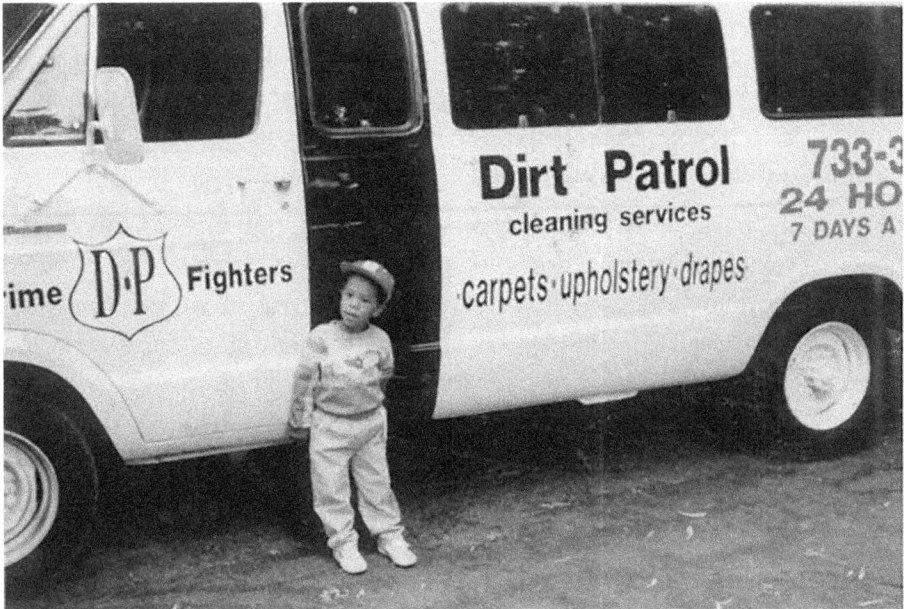

Start a Business

I was the Chief Grime Fighter for my company, the Dirt Patrol. We fought grime, not crime. My nephew, Omari, guards the truck. *Los Angeles, California, 1988*

Success can arise from difficult circumstances. Stay focused on solutions and a positive outcome. Negative thinking will lead to negative results. Continue to visualize success even in the midst of a great struggle.

PRODUCTIVITY AND SELF-ESTEEM

To truly be educated and empowered, you must have the ability to create, the ability to actualize your dream. This ability is predicated on healthy self-esteem. Building positive, yet balanced self-esteem is an evolutionary process that progresses with each project and activity we undertake and with each challenge we overcome. To have healthy self-esteem is to have a sense of dignity, independence, self-love, confidence, and self-respect. We build our self-esteem by becoming productive.

In order to become a creator—someone who can take a thought or a dream and make it a reality—belief in yourself is essential. You must believe that you can overcome obstacles. The activity or endeavor is unimportant; facing the difficulties is critical in developing your self-esteem and creative powers.

For me, basketball played a central role in building positive self-esteem. As a child I was not very good in sports. When games were organized on my neighborhood street, neither the boys nor the girls would let me play football or baseball with them. I remember going home one day, lying on my bed, and thinking that I would focus on basketball. I decided I would practice until I could beat all the other boys and girls in my neighborhood.

During my first season in the YMCA league with the "Hot Shots" basketball team, I only took one shot: an air ball. I needed a lot of work. I focused and practiced. I can recall playing the radio and shooting baskets in the backyard until late in the night. Basketball became my best friend. On Friday and Saturday nights, if I could get access to our school gym, I would bring in my music and a ball and practice for hours. I was in basketball heaven. A friend's father would train his two sons and me at the local YMCA at five o'clock in the morning before school. A teacher at school even let me bring a ball to class during tests.

Despite all my efforts, during my first year in high school my team finished with a record of three wins and twenty-three losses. I was convinced that we had figured out every way to lose. After that, I spent more time alone in the gym with just my music and a ball. I struggled to master the skills, but also loved every minute.

Later, in my last two years of high school, we won sixty games and lost only three. We won the Southern California championship for small schools. The *Los Angeles Times* and other newspapers honored me.

After I was named Southern California's Player of the Year for small schools, someone complimented me by saying how "lucky" I was to win the award. I thought, "Lucky? If he only knew how much I had to practice." Basketball did not come easily. I loved it, struggled, focused, and was able to enjoy success. In the process, I was building positive self-esteem because, despite all else, deep down I knew I was a ballplayer.

Through the process of facing and overcoming adversity, you gain confidence and believe that you are stronger than your obstacles. Struggles are a blessing in disguise. If you stay the course, you can emerge from the challenge with a greater belief in yourself. The thought, "Yes, I can" is a powerful belief. This thought, coupled with unflinching action, will inspire you to proceed to your dream and not be deterred by obstacles and opposition.

Living your dream demands that you believe, "Yes, I can." Challenge yourself with new activities. You may not do well initially. Work at it and once you overcome the challenge, you too will gain the "Yes, I can" belief. Overcoming difficulties is the road to gaining this critical belief in yourself.

SACRIFICE

Choose your dream carefully. You had better want it badly.

Like a mother giving birth, you will have to push past pain to turn your vision into a reality.

No matter how great or small your dream, realizing your vision requires sacrifice. What are you willing to sacrifice to realize your vision? Money... pride...time? Depending on how challenging the dream is, realizing your vision may not be easy.

What are you willing to give up to realize your vision?

FOCUS

Focus means sacrifice. If your vision is what you truly desire, focusing on it and sacrificing for its realization should be a labor of love. Your time, mind, and desire will have to laser in on your vision to make it a reality.

The focused mind reaches the destination.

Struggles can produce benefits that will only emerge under the
challenge of a difficult situation.

Whether faced with unemployment or how to carry on without resources,
tap into your creative genius for answers.

Your God will send you ideas.

FAILURE: WHAT A BLESSING

Struggle often involves facing setbacks and failures. We often look down on someone who fails. If we fail ourselves, we run from the experience, ashamed.

When we fail at something, the experience is rich in lessons that we could not have known before the endeavor. If we had known them earlier, we would have acted differently. Failure should not be a source of embarrassment, but a learning opportunity. Struggle and failures are our classrooms. Disappointments and failures will happen. Mistakes are good. Study them, stay positive, but always stay in motion. Learn their lessons, but continue to move on and graduate to new challenges.

Select an activity or project. Do something,
even if it is a simple endeavor.

Just get started.

The process will build self-esteem.

Belief in yourself will empower you to obtain your life's dream.

CHAPTER 10

Sometimes You Just Have to Have Faith

"The proof that one truly believes is in action."
—Bayard Rustin

"We do not need more intellectual power, we need more spiritual power. We do not need more of the things that are seen, we need more of the things that are unseen."
—Calvin Coolidge

Faith is not simply saying, "I believe" or even attending religious services. Faith is taking action in the face of obstacles and the unknown. Faith is striving to achieve a result that you feel is greater than you alone. Build your faith by taking on a challenge. The lack of faith can cloud your thoughts with fear and doubt. Great achievements are fueled by great faith.

Following graduation from Columbia, I applied for a Ford Foundation grant to research youth development in Zimbabwe, a former British colony on the northern border of South Africa. A professor told me that he had been to Zimbabwe, knew officials in the government, and would arrange for my accommodations and a job teaching in a school. Prior to leaving the United States, I had arranged to visit relatives in several states before making the journey to Africa. As no one in my family had traveled to Africa, I felt like a hero. Unfortunately, the night before I was to leave for Zimbabwe, my professor advised me that he was unable to arrange for a job or a place to live. Faced with the humiliation of returning home or facing the unknown and going to Africa, I decided I had to go. A friend gave me addresses of people she knew in Zimbabwe. I left New York not telling my family that I had no idea where I was going and what I was going to do once I got there.

I arrived in Zimbabwe with the addresses and a postcard from my friend, Penny Andrews, who wrote: "Please accommodate [Daniel] for a few nights. His arrangements weren't concluded, and I'd hate him to be left on the streets."

Sometimes You Just Gotta Have Faith

I traveled to Zimbabwe for a nine-month stay without a place to stay or job, only this card from a friend. *1984*

When I arrived in Zimbabwe, I gathered my luggage, went through customs, and got a taxi. I asked to be taken to the address on the card my friend had given me. When I arrived at the house, I found no one home. I went next door to find out if they knew when their neighbors would be returning. The next-door neighbor told me that they would be gone for a month. "Great," I thought, "I'm in Africa and stuck. I know no one in this city, country, or continent!" The neighbor, James Logan, a white man, asked me where I was from. I said, "Los Angeles." He told me he was from Hollywood, California, and had been living in Zimbabwe, previously Rhodesia, for thirteen years. He said I could stay at his house for the next month.

Things have a way of working out. Sometimes you just have to have faith.

I was disappointed when I got out and saw the capital city, Harare. I was expecting something exotic—lions, giraffes, and zebras. Instead, I saw what looked like a mid-size American city—buildings, parks, traffic, restaurants, and hotels.

I soon learned that I was not "black" in Zimbabwe, but there I was considered to be "colored" or of mixed race. Zimbabwe, when it was the colonial state of Rhodesia, had a system of government that divided people by race—whites, coloreds, and blacks. One white man, who saw me as colored, told me how much he hated blacks. I was upset at first, but when I realized that he did not see me as black, I thought that distinction could prove to be quite interesting.

My grant proposal to the Ford Foundation was for me to teach in a school. A government official informed me that I had to be sponsored by a government agency. However, I found out later that the Education Ministry was not interested in utilizing me as a teacher. Once the Ministry of Youth, Sport, and Culture learned that I knew how to play basketball, they were eager for me to put on clinics throughout the country. So I conducted my study on schools and youth development while coaching basketball.

Zimbabwe was a former British Colony, and this influence remained. At around 2 p.m. one day, I was teaching about 100 players how to play defense. Then a jet-black man, with a clipped British accent, walked into the middle of my clinic and announced, "Tea time, sir." He proceeded to serve me tea and crumpets on the basketball court. Although I was not a tea drinker, I thought it was so funny that I had to stand there and sip tea "as a proper gentleman" before returning to my clinic.

At the end of my year in Zimbabwe, my uncle, Dr. Fred Kennedy, contacted me to tell me that his friend, Marques Haynes, a former Harlem Globetrotter and NBA Hall of Famer, wanted to donate basketball shoes to one of the basketball teams that I was coaching. After several telephone conversations, I recommended that Haynes bring his new team, the Harlem Magicians, to Zimbabwe. He could then donate the shoes personally. His team could put on teaching clinics and exhibition games. Haynes agreed with the idea. If I could raise the money, including round-trip airfare, and organize a tour, Marques Haynes and the Harlem Magicians would come.

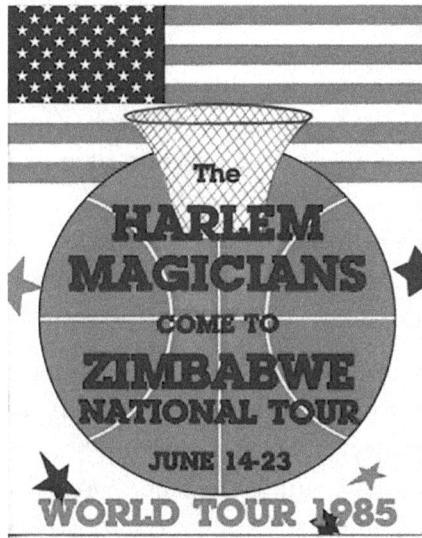

Harlem Magicians Come to Zimbabwe National Tour Program

Former Harlem Globetrotter and NBA Hall of Famer Marcus Haynes agreed to come to Zimbabwe if I could raise the money. Working from the floor of the U.S. Information Service offices and with no resources except a typewriter, phone, and phone book, I raised over $50,000 in cash and services.

During this time, because I had come to know the staff at the United States Information Center, a secretary there said I could use a corner of her desk to work. Although I was grateful, that corner shortly became too confining. So I set up shop on the floor of the information center. Armed with a typewriter, phone book, and a telephone, I began the process of contacting and signing up sponsors. "The Harlem Magicians Come to Zimbabwe National Tour" was a tremendous success. Zimbabwean government officials told me that opening night, which was attended by more than 5,000 fans, was the largest social gathering of whites, coloreds, and blacks in the then brief history of that once racially divided nation.

Marques Haynes and the Harlem Magicians basketball team arrive in Zimbabwe. Here I am welcoming team representative **Dr. Fred Kennedy**. The tour resulted in the largest multiracial social gathering at that point in the young nation's history, following nearly 20 years of civil war.
Harare, Zimbabwe, June 14, 1985 (Photo by Howard Bingham)

I raised $50,000 in cash and services from companies in Zimbabwe in order to bring the team over. I found a tree, in this case, the floor, and I got started. All the resources I needed came after I started with what I had. Who could have imagined when I arrived in Zimbabwe with nowhere to stay that my time there would end with the success of the tour?

Sometimes you just have to have faith.

How are you putting your faith to work?

They Found Their Tree
$25 and a Dream of Going to Africa
by Anita White

My daughter, Andrea, was sixteen years old when she got involved with Find A Tree through the Young Black Scholars program, and she wanted to go to Africa. I personally did not think that she was going to get to go to Africa, when I asked her, "Andrea, how much money do you have?" She was like, "Mom, I have $25." I responded, in disbelief, "$25? You cannot go to Africa with $25!"

One of her first Find A Tree projects was to start her catering business. She first wanted to be a caterer, so she started by making peach cobblers. Through catering, she raised the money to go to Africa. She raised more than $3,500 through sponsorships and her catering business. Andrea recalled, "Mr. Armstrong had everyone in the classes write down their dream. My dream was to have my own catering business. I formed a partnership with another student in the Find A Tree program from Young Black Scholars, and we had our first job within a week. It was wonderful, learning what it took to have my own business, but I wanted more."

She decided she wanted to go to Africa with only $25. That is faith. She used scripture as the basis for her going to Africa so she could have a direction, and she prayed every day. She found Bible scripture. One was Habakkuk 2:2, "Write down the vision and make it plain." Andrea had to have a vision: going to Africa. Andrea stated in an interview that she first thought of going to

Africa when, "During one of our Saturday Find A Tree classes, I overheard Mr. Armstrong telling another group of students about a teacher from Crenshaw High School, who took students to Africa. Mr. Armstrong shared with students how this teacher and her students donated books and school supplies on their trips to Africa. When I heard that I thought to myself, 'This is something that I want to do.' I wanted to use my life to make a difference in the lives of people. I knew that I wanted to be a part of such a group. I had always dreamed of helping others and to see the world, so I thought, 'Why not start now?'"

Andrea's going to Africa changed her life completely. Going to Africa was wonderful for her because it gave her a new outlook on life. Andrea saw the poverty and how hard life was for the people there. It changed her completely. When she came home, I really had little or no trouble with her. She was wonderful. It took two years to get her to shop for new things. Andrea saw the poverty there, and she felt that the things she had were good enough. So going to Africa made her appreciate her life. The experience made her appreciate her family. It made her appreciate the education she had. It made her want to do better and be better. It made her want to become an engineer and improve the city that she lives in, so she is in college now and wants to improve her community. I do not think all that would have happened, and she would not have appreciated life if she had not gone to Africa and if she had not had an opportunity to be a part of the Find A Tree program. If Find A Tree did not help anyone else, it helped my daughter tremendously. It was wonderful seeing Andrea before Find A Tree and seeing the

Andrea who is in college now, focused on what she wants to become. The seeds started with Find A Tree. Find A Tree enriched her life. It made her think more clearly as she followed the steps in the book. She has passed the book on to another student. The things she learned she passed on, so one thing for sure she learned was to learn it and pass it on to the next person.

CHAPTER 11

Create Opportunities through Service

"Everybody can be great because anybody can serve."
—Martin Luther King, Jr.

TALENT + SERVICE = A LIFETIME OF OPPORTUNITIES

Life's opportunities and resources open their doors to you if you pursue your dream and use your talents and gifts to serve others. Opportunities to do what you never believed possible will come to you.

I have tried to live by these principles. This practice has provided me with a lifetime of opportunities and empowered me to live my dream.

I love to organize. This is my gift. By utilizing my gift as an organizer, I not only have learned and improved my skills, but also each circumstance has led to another more challenging opportunity. Living your dream is a process. The starting point can often be working for no compensation or without the prospect of anything more promising. Along the journey there are struggles, sacrifices, and growth. En route, you gain the faith required to live and achieve your dream. If you get started on the path to accomplishing your dream, you never know what may await you.

My work with the Coalition for a Free South Africa while an undergraduate student at Columbia required that I work closely with the dean, Dr. Robert Pollack, and other university officials as we worked to resolve the issue of South African investments. Later when I was in graduate school at UCLA, Dr. Pollack asked a Columbia alumnus to assist me in my career. The alumnus, an entertainment lawyer, and I met to discuss my interest in the music business. The alumnus referred me to the president of A&M Records, then the nation's largest privately owned record company. The president of A&M, Gil Friesen, hired me as his executive assistant. Working at A&M exposed me to the entertainment business. A&M was exciting because I got great seats at concerts, free CDs, tickets to the Grammy Awards, and opportunities to meet the artists. This job was a great and unexpected opportunity that came my way as a result of my work at Columbia on the issue of divestment. Ultimately, I could not keep up in business and law school and work at A&M at the same time, so I had to resign my position.

Unique opportunities can come your way when you give of yourself in service. The opportunity I had at A&M was not advertised, but opportunities can be created by being proactive and being willing to give of yourself in service.

One of the best ways to start living your dream is to figure out how others can benefit from your talents. How can you serve humanity? There are fewer roadblocks if you begin in a spirit of service to others.

CHAPTER 12

Value People

"To be nobody—but yourself in a world which is doing its best, night and day, to make you everybody but yourself—means to fight the hardest battle which any human being can fight—and never stop fighting."

—e.e. cummings

THE ROAD TO SUCCESS: PEOPLE

Nearly all you want to do, be, or have will come through another person. The people you meet are some of your most important resources. Take the time to see and listen to the people around you. They are there for a reason, and they can help you to manifest your dream.

Courtesy. Respect. Appreciation. Listening. Caring. Giving. Honoring. Remembering. Humility. These basic principles build positive human relations, and their development leads you down the road to success.

You build your business by using these principles of human relations. They apply when relating to your customers.

These are the people who will bring you money and promote your business by telling others about you and your business. Again, positive human relations are your road to success. No one is "unimportant." All people have value. Search and you will find it.

As a student athlete at Columbia University, I often wanted to shoot baskets early in the morning or late at night. Although I had a good relationship with the athletic director and his administrative staff, the most important person for me was the janitor. He controlled the building early in the morning and late at night, and he had the keys to the gym. The athletic director could do little to help me pursue my dream; it was the janitor who "held the key." Respect all people. We can help each other realize our dreams.

HUMAN RELATIONS

When you meet someone, ask for his or her business card or contact information. When networking, think of ways you can help the people you meet. Think about ways you can help them to succeed. Can you send them a referral or an interesting news article? Help others, and help will come your way in return.

TEAMWORK

At some point in the development of your project, you may have to bring others on board to form a team. Many projects and businesses fail, not because of a lack of ingenuity in the concept or product, but because of a breakdown in human relations. Team members' talents should complement one another. This unity enables the team to move forward to realize their collective vision.

Before involving potential new team members, the prospective members should discuss the following points:

1. The abilities and talents that will be needed

2. What each member offers toward the realization of the project

3. The level of involvement in terms of time, sacrifice, and standards that will be required and expected of team members

4. Conflict resolution procedures within the team

5. Decision-making procedures

6. Team members' roles and responsibilities

These terms should be put in writing and signed by all members. This formality may seem too troublesome, but as the project or business evolves, this record may prove to be valuable.

Read Dale Carnegie's classic:
How to Win Friends & Influence People

They Found Their Tree
From Lock-Up to Beverly Hills
The Darwin Ramirez Story

One of the birthplaces of the Find A Tree program was at the California Youth Authority's Fred C. Nelles Youth Correctional Institution in Whittier, California. Since the Find A Tree program was at Nelles for nearly one year, there are many stories that come from that environment. This piece illustrates my experience at Nelles seen through the story of Darwin Ramirez.

* * *

Darwin Ramirez was raised by a single mother who, because she worked two jobs, often left him to watch his two younger brothers. By age nine, Darwin began to associate with and admire members of various local gangs. Fighting, stealing, and rebelling against authority soon became a way of life for him.

One day before a gang fight, Darwin and his girlfriend were with other gang members in a local park. The other gang members threw their gang signs. Darwin responded with his own. A fight quickly ensued. Darwin and fellow gang members ran the other gang members out of the park. Upset, Darwin went home and got a gun. He went out looking for rival gang members. Darwin found a group of guys from another gang and shot at them. One person was hit. Darwin and his friends got away.

Still upset from the previous fight, the next day he went out again, armed and looking for rival gang members. After a brief fight with a group of rivals, Darwin shot one of them. Darwin recalled,

"At that time in my life, I did not care about anything. The only thing I cared about was my gang."

This time he was arrested and incarcerated for attempted murder. At age fourteen, Darwin was sentenced to fourteen years and eight months at the California Youth Authority's Fred C. Nelles Youth Correctional Institution.

At Nelles, Darwin continued to promote gang activity. Fighting rival gang members was his favorite pastime. He used his considerable leadership skills to maintain gang members' rules and traditions—"jailhouse rules."

Darwin was sent to lock-down—a one-room isolation cell for disruptive inmates. In lock-down, inmates or "wards," as they are called by the state, were kept in a room by themselves or sometimes two in a room for twenty-three hours a day. Inmates showered in a cage. He spent a year under these conditions. Once Darwin got a roommate, and they "fought until they could not lift their arms anymore," according to Darwin.

While in lock-down, Darwin was elevated by his peers to "shot caller"—a position of honor for a gang leader. After a year in lock-down, he was moved to Adams Cottage. Darwin tried to exert his newfound leadership role as a shot caller by establishing the jailhouse rules in Adams Cottage. He initiated and encouraged fights and rebellious behavior, and he exacerbated racial tension. The staff, under the leadership of Derek Finks, disciplined Darwin continuously. He was denied all personal property, given limited recreation time, and was required to be in bed by 7 p.m.

He soon recognized that his agenda would not be tolerated in Adams Cottage. Through the considerable influence of Mr. Finks and the Adams Cottage staff, he began to conform to the institution's rules. The young inmate earned rewards for good behavior: to have a room, get mail, and stay up until 9:30 p.m.

Darwin found that he enjoyed the benefits of living within the law. However, rival gang members at Nelles knew of his past and continued to attack him when he interacted with other young men at the institution's school.

In August of 1999, Mr. Finks told the wards that a new program was coming to Adams called Find A Tree. Nearly forty wards signed up for the program, but only twenty could enroll. After undergoing an extensive interview with Finks, Darwin was selected for the program.

Darwin realized immediately that he could learn a great deal from the Find A Tree program. He felt the program could take him to "another level in his life." He also recognized that he had to heal from the emotional scars of his life. In one class period, Darwin shared with the class the story of the day he was to meet his father and how his father rejected him. In front of his peers and former rivals, Darwin shamelessly cried. The shot caller shared his heart and pain.

Find A Tree classes included basketball training where Darwin learned how to deal with people as teammates on the basketball court. At an initial training session, I stopped practice when I sensed that the mood had suddenly changed. I asked, "What is going on?" After a long pause, Darwin stepped forward, pointed to another player on the court, and announced, "This jerk stepped on my foot, and I've gotta knock his ass out." Practice was adjourned for an on-the-court session on human relations. Darwin got the point and apologized.

In the Find A Tree class, students discussed character, the necessity of struggle, time management, and writing a plan of action. At one point the students did not complete a major assignment, which was to write their personal plan of action for how they were going to pursue their dream in jail and upon their release, despite having a month to work on it. In response to their lack of motivation, I informed the class that "I could not help people who did not want to help themselves."

I abruptly announced my departure and indicated that there was nothing more that I could do for them. Many expressed their disappointment and their sense of betrayal in this decision. One student said, "Every time I find myself liking someone, they walk out…just like my dad… He walked out on me too." Another said, "Go ahead and leave… You shouldn't have come here anyway! You know we are criminals, and we don't like to write!" Darwin recalled, "When Mr. Armstrong walked out on us I was hurt, but I had to put on my mask—that jailhouse mask that you always have so you do not let anyone know what you are feeling. A lot of us in the class put that mask on when Mr. Armstrong left. We were mad, but we just acted like we did not care." The next day, the students met with Mr. Finks, their senior counselor, to discuss their anger with me. Mr. Finks explained the importance of putting their thoughts on paper. Many participants recognized that they had not been giving their best effort to the program. That night the students worked until 3 a.m. on their assignment. They continued to write for the next five days, sometimes in the shower area when no other space was available. Darwin demonstrated his proficiency at writing and working on the computer as he helped and guided others with how to write their plans. Five days after my departure, I returned to the class where the students presented well-conceived plans of action. Impressed, I said that I would do all I could to help them. The students apologized for their lack of motivation in the past and pledged to work harder in the future. The students, staff, and I embraced. Some cried. Darwin said, "When we got together with Mr. Armstrong again, we let loose. No one could keep on the mask that hid our feelings anymore. We let out our true feelings." Following this renewed commitment,

Darwin called on his fellow students to organize themselves. He ran for president of Find A Tree at Nelles and won. Darwin recalled, "When I got that position, that was the best feeling. I was feeling the glory. I felt like I did something good. Then I started helping other people write their plans of action for their dreams. This made me feel better and better about myself. But I ended up getting a big head. By the time I got out, I was so confident that I felt I could do anything."

Darwin's natural leadership skills developed as he encouraged the group to work as a team and help each other pursue their dreams—despite racial differences, gang affiliation, and being in jail. Ramirez said later, "I once lived a corrupt life, which led me [to Nelles]. The Find A Tree program [gave] me a different point of view in life. It opened my eyes and let me realize that there is more to life than just living a gang life. It gave me the opportunity to realize that I have a dream, and that I can achieve it if I give myself the chance."

On May 2, 2000, Darwin Ramirez was released from Nelles and immediately called me. I referred him to Jaleesa Hazzard, the executive director of a youth entertainment industry summer jobs program. Hazzard had met Darwin and the Find A Tree class members when she visited Nelles as a guest speaker.

Recalling the experience, Hazzard stated, "The experience we had that first night was extremely interesting. Not knowing what to expect, we sat down with the group. Instead of hardened criminals, they were very focused, communicative, and articulate regarding their own personal goals, and they were anxious to learn whatever we had to offer. I got to know Darwin Ramirez, the leader of the group, who boldly asked me, after hearing what I did, if I would help him when he got out in a few months. Darwin is a prime example of what I think Find A Tree can do for a young person.

"Darwin Ramirez is probably a natural leader, but in his past life he did know how to use this talent in a constructive way. He also had no focus or outlet for his considerable talents and felt powerless to resist the negative forces in his environment. He used his energy for the wrong things, and this practice eventually led him to criminal behavior, the wrong friends, absence from school, and Nelles. However, when he was there, he was lucky enough to become a part of Find A Tree, and he found himself and a plan of action that could change his life. By the time I met him, the light had come on in his eyes, and he was ready to take some positive steps to change his life.

"When Darwin was released, as promised, he called me. As promised, I agreed to see him and to help him if he would stick to his plans. He first did his community service hours with me. He immediately became a valuable part of our office, and I think he began to realize that the lessons he had learned through Find A Tree would serve him out in the real world. He always did his absolute best; nothing short of excellence was good enough for him, and he was on time, focused, and responsible well beyond his years. He put in extra time, and we worked with him on writing a resume and had him apply for our summer program. There were no promises, and he competed with other students from Los Angeles. He secured a job for the summer with BMG Entertainment in the Human Resources/Facilities Department. Their assessment of his work was much like mine. They have been employers of our program for ten years and were quick to say that he was the best student they had ever had. When a permanent position became open in one of their subsidiaries, they referred Darwin with no reservations. He got the job and was a full-time employee with a decent salary, benefits, and a real chance to pursue his dream of a career in entertainment."

After working at BMG's subsidiary, Killer Tracks, for over a year, Darwin Ramirez violated his parole terms and returned to jail for six months. He was released and returned to working in the entertainment industry for a television production company. Darwin said of his saga, "I have gone through struggle and failure, and now I am trying to get to where I was the first time I got out of Nelles. I am working as hard as I can to live my dream."

One of the lessons to be learned from Darwin is the importance of your associations, particularly if you are attempting to turn your life around. Living your dream may require breaking off close ties with friends and even family members if being in their company is detrimental to your development and progress.

Living your dream is like climbing a mountain. In pursuing your goals, you may fall. The test will be your ability to get back up and climb again. Darwin fell. He has gotten back up and is striving to reach his dream and potential. Ultimately, Darwin's test will be his ability to learn from the mistakes that caused him to fall and correct them as he climbs the mountain of his dreams.

DARWIN RAMIREZ UPDATE

Since 2003, Darwin has worked in the field of social services. As of June 2014, he works for a non-profit agency assisting under-privileged youth who come from low-income families in violence-plagued communities.

"Find A Tree was a life changer for me, no matter how bad my situation or how many times I fell. With Find A Tree as my foundation, I was able to rebuild my life. Thank you Find A Tree."

- Darwin Ramirez

CHAPTER 13

Plan, Prioritize, and Manage Your Time

*"Your time is limited, so don't waste
it living someone else's life."*
—Steve Jobs

NINE STEPS: FROM DREAM TO REALITY

Step 1: Dream

A dream is a mental concept of what you want to do or achieve. Do not limit your dream to what is "realistic" in your mind. Imagine an impossible dream. To dream is free. Splurge.

Step 2: Vision

A vision is a clear picture, as detailed as possible in your mind, of what you want to do and what the end product will look like. Visualize success.

Lie in your bed or sit in a comfortable chair. Close your eyes.

See yourself performing the tasks that your dream will require. See how you are dressed and how you interact with others; see yourself living your dream. Imagination and visualization are critical initial steps in the creative process.

Your thoughts are powerful. Use and direct your power by focusing your thoughts into a vivid vision of what you intend to achieve.

Step 3: Faith, Determination, and Knowledge

These qualities are the spirit, state of mind, and information needed to commence your journey. Faith in your God and yourself that, yes, you can make your vision a reality, are critical to success, even if your dream seems more like wishful thinking. Determination will energize and motivate you to overcome obstacles. Information and knowledge will enable you to make intelligent decisions and move forward. Your mind is your greatest asset. Your determination, faith in the unseen, and ability to educate yourself through research and study will be the critical factors in giving birth to your dream. To live your dream, you must have all three—faith, determination, and knowledge.

Step 4: A Plan of Action

A plan of action is a well thought out road map. Be prepared for change but begin with a plan of action. An effective plan is one that is realistic. Take into consideration the real-life circumstances that will have to be overcome. Plan for the unexpected. Ultimately, your God or Supreme Being will guide you, but first you have to do your part.

Many have a dream, vision, the necessary desire, and will, but few take the time to write out a plan. The vision, once on paper in the form of a plan, brings you a step closer to the reality. A dream on paper in the form of a plan makes your vision tangible.

A plan is a road map. All events and circumstances will not occur exactly as we foresee. The planning process will require that the vision be clarified, defined, and tested in theory before making it a reality. Anticipate potential problems or obstacles you may encounter when carrying out your plan. An effective plan does not pretend that the world is perfect and all will go as expected. The ability to anticipate problems and prepare for unexpected changes is critical to writing a useful plan. Identify the obstacles you may encounter and write down strategies to overcome those roadblocks. The plan should be carefully crafted so that you can follow each step in the time allocated. An effective plan is a realistic series of steps, a useful guide, and a gauge of progress.

Planning requires visualizing what needs to be done, mathematical calculation of the resources that will be needed, the time frame required to assemble the component parts, and a creative mind to imagine how to overcome problems. These attributes—visualization, calculation, time management, and imagination—are all qualities of a creator.

Step 5: One-Year Goals

Describe in real terms what you want to achieve over the next year. Use dates and figures whenever possible.

Step 6: Monthly Goals

Describe in real terms what you want to accomplish each month/quarter. These goals should tie into your year-end goals. Use dates and figures whenever possible.

Step 7: Weekly Goals and Priorities

Determine the tasks you must accomplish this week and every week for the current month. Collectively, these priorities should enable you to meet all of your goals for the month.

Step 8: Daily Priorities

Determine the tasks you must complete today. Be realistic. If you can only get one thing done, do that one thing. The key is to complete your daily priorities. These tasks are the building blocks to making your dream a reality.

Step 9: Time Management

Time management is your plan for the day—when and how long you will take to carry out each item on your schedule. If watching the game is not on your schedule, you have to decide: game or dream? If you consistently fulfill your daily priorities and stay on your time management schedule, your dream will begin to take form. Success will come when you effectively plan and effectively utilize your time each day.

We all are given the same amount of time in a day. How efficiently you accomplish your tasks and priorities determines whether you make progress or fall into stagnation.

Time management is like writing a daily plan of action. Think it through, recognize that unforeseen events can and do occur, and plan accordingly. The better you are able to plan your time and accomplish your tasks, the more effective you will be in realizing your dream.

This type of scheduling may at first seem excessive. However, if you have a lot to do, and want to maximize efficiency and reduce stress, a time management plan is critical. Be as detailed as possible. Plan for time to relax, take a walk, etc. Be realistic in what you know you can get done in a day. If your day has a number of occurrences that cannot be preplanned, factor them into your schedule. The key is to complete your priorities despite the constant changes in your day.

With proper planning, stress is reduced. You have already thought through your day or week. Having planned it out, you know that if you follow your schedule, all will get done.

If your already hectic schedule will only permit you to get one task completed on your project in a day, complete that one item. Each step, no matter how small, moves your dream closer to becoming a reality. With detailed daily planning and by staying on schedule, you can find the ten or twenty minutes needed to get your project's task done while fulfilling other commitments. As you accomplish each day's and week's priorities, your vision and dream will gradually begin to take shape.

This is planning. It has to be realistic, with the aim of increasing productivity and efficiency. This is time management.

Begin your time management schedule by listing your project priorities for the week, along with your regular, established activities. In your weekly planner, write in the activity and timeframe for your established activities. Then, map out the days and times you will need to carry out your week's tasks. All will not work out as expected; plan time for the unforeseen. Once your plan is written, you should know before the week's start where you should be by the week's end, and whether it will be possible to carry out all that you hoped to accomplish.

At week's end, study your effectiveness in meeting your priorities and time schedule. Make corrections in the planning of your daily activities to become more successful in later weeks at completing all of your priorities.

Sample Daily Schedule

AM

6:30	Rise
6:30-7:00	Stretch, in-home exercises, and meditation
7:00-7:30	Shower and dress
7:30-8:00	Eat breakfast and review the day's schedule
8:00-8:40	Travel to work
8:45-9:00	Outline topics for project proposal
9:00-10:30	Work
10:30-10:45	Review project topics
10:45-12:30	Work

PM

12:30-1:00	Work on proposal while having lunch
1:00-5:00	Work

Daniel Armstrong

5:00-6:00	Travel home
6:00-6:45	Relax and read email
6:45-8:00	Dinner
8:00	Finalize project proposal topics
8:30	Return phone calls
9:00	Read *How to Live Your Dreams: Find a Tree and Get Started* (again)
10:00	Bed

CHAPTER 14

Distinguish Yourself with Excellence

"Details make the difference between a champion and a near champion."

—John Wooden

"Some people aren't used to an environment where excellence is expected."

—Steve Jobs

Coach John Wooden won ten national basketball championships while coaching at UCLA. His teams won 88 straight games at one point, and he is considered one of the sport's greatest coaches. Coach Wooden was meticulous. The first lesson he taught his athletes at the start of each season was how to put on their socks correctly in order to prevent blisters. Blisters, Wooden figured, would detract from a player's ability to perform and, therefore, hurt the team. This example shows the meticulous approach of the most successful coach in the history of college basketball.

Distinguish Yourself with Excellence

Former UCLA coach John Wooden and me. *Pasadena, California, 2002*

Excellence comes only when you are meticulous. When others are exhausted and are prepared to say, "That's good enough," "It doesn't matter," or "No one will notice," that is the time that the champion must examine a play or a document one more time in order to perfect the details.

You must strive for excellence in the project, program, or skill you undertake. Pursuing excellence is like mining the gold and diamonds buried deep inside of you.

Excellence means to "stand out," to "excel." By nurturing and perfecting your gifts, you are manifesting the talents and gifts implanted in you. Many have latent talents that they have never unearthed or shared. If they developed their gifts and shared them, they would then stand out.

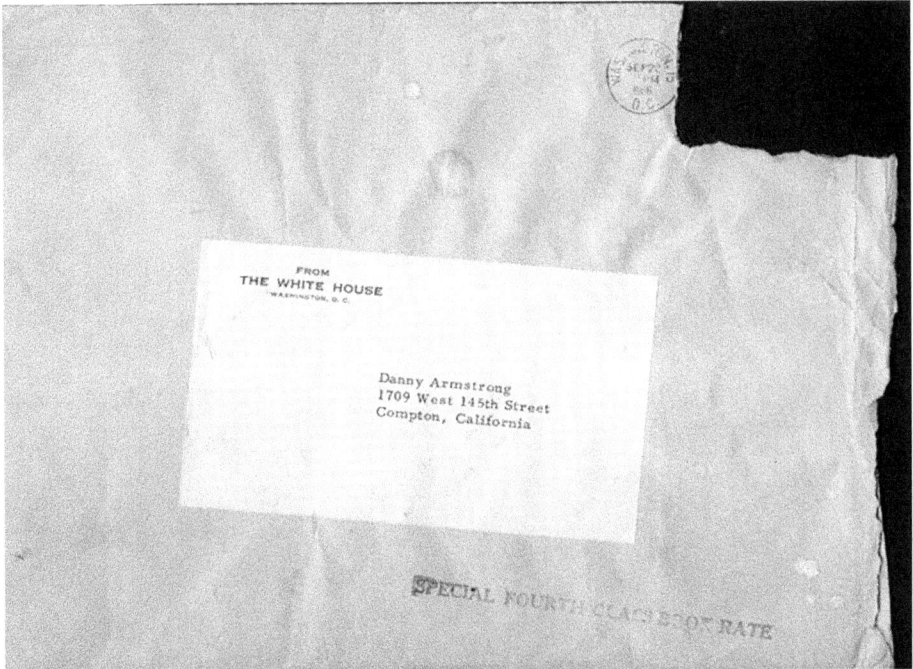

Identify What You Are Passionate About, Your Interests, Talents, and Gifts

My passion for politics started early. At age three-and-a-half years, I dictated a letter to my mother for then U.S. President Lyndon Johnson. Here is the envelope that the White House's response came in. *Compton, California, 1966*

Excellence will come if you persistently toil and polish your talents. Struggle is similar to the pressure and friction applied when polishing silver. Struggle will polish your talents and gifts. Polish your gifts, manifest excellence, and you will stand out and shine before the world.

CHAPTER 15

Understand the Process:
From a Seed to a Tree

"The two most important days in your life are the day you are born…and the day you find out why."

—*Mark Twain*

Human life evolves from one stage to the next: from a thought, to sperm and an egg, to an embryo, to a baby, to a child, to a teenager, and to an adult. At each stage, we learn valuable lessons that we need for the next stage of development.

Your project will often start small as well: a seed, a thought, planted in your fertile mind. As your project evolves, sprouts, and grows, learn the valuable lessons at each stage. You are going to have to push through the obstacles that lie in your way. Although we often want overnight success, gradual progress allows us to learn, grow, and understand each stage of development. The struggle to realize your dream when your resources appear limited draws out your creative genius that is buried deep inside you. Many point to lack of money as their problem. If you have money but do not use your creative mind, your money will be wasted. If you recognize and develop your creative genius to overcome obstacles, your seed or idea will soon sprout and grow into a tree.

An example of taking a seed or an idea and nurturing it is Beverly Silverstein, a dynamic and motivated teacher at Crenshaw High School in Los Angeles. Silverstein invited me to speak to her class about my experiences in Africa. For the students of this urban high school, traveling to Africa may have seemed like traveling to the moon. I invited the students to travel with me on my next trip by establishing pen pals in Ghana. With the encouragement of their teacher, the students wrote letters, and I delivered them. Later, after exchanging several letters with their Ghanaian counterparts, the students decided that they would like to go to Ghana to meet their pen pals.

Without waiting for a grant or free airline tickets, the students had bake sales, raffles, and car washes to raise money for their trip to Africa. They raised the necessary amount of money and went to Ghana. They returned enlightened by their experience and empowered, knowing that they could make a dream into reality. Later that year, when the president of Ghana visited Los Angeles, these students were invited to meet and attend a luncheon with the president. Silverstein has since taken her class to Ghana every year. This teacher and her students are examples of living their dream by finding a tree and getting started.

So often we dream and want the final result immediately. Focus on what you can do today, although that action is not the intended result. Continue to build on that initial action, and the end result will come in time.

Start small.

Learn the lessons of each stage of development.

The struggle to grow will produce a tree secured in a foundation of faith, knowledge, wisdom, and understanding.

CHAPTER 16

Tap into Your Creative Genius

"Act boldly and unseen forces will come to your aid."
—Dorothea Brande

YOUR CREATIVE POWER

Thoughts, ideas, and dreams shape the physical reality that you see. They are the basis of your creative power. Valuing your thoughts, ideas, and dreams, which are all tied into your self-esteem, is essential for giving birth to projects, programs, and inventions that can contribute to making a better world. Individuals who achieve success in life and realize their goals respect their thoughts and intuition; they plan, struggle, focus, and sacrifice to realize their dreams. The ability to translate your dreams into reality is creative power.

People who are underachievers and who blame others for their problems have lost the ability to dream. They usually do not respect their own dreams, instead discounting them as unrealistic. They also have not developed the psychological, spiritual, and educational tools needed to make their dreams or ideas a reality. When we do not use our creative power, we become slaves to jobs and bosses that we do not enjoy and slaves to circumstances that we feel we are unable to change.

We are often told why our plans will not work. The unfocused mind will cease to dream with this discouragement. The creative mind sees past the difficulties and focuses on the dream's components; step-by-step addressing each obstacle as it arises. Visualize the end product and remain determined to ultimately reach your destination.

Musical Genius: Stevie Wonder

Stevie Wonder and I are at the funeral for **Syreeta Wright**, who was a great friend and supporter of Find A Tree. *Los Angeles, California, July 13, 2004* (Photo by Malcom Shabazz)

We are all born with creative powers that, when fully developed, make us one with the Creator. Activating your creative power helps you live your dream. Think a thought and make it happen.

What would you attempt to do if you knew you were destined to succeed?

Find a tree and get started.

CHAPTER 17

You Will Achieve What You Expect and Try

"In order to win, you must expect to win."
—Dan Fouts

"I need money to get started."

"I do not have the money."

"I have never done that before."

"I have never studied or trained for that."

"What will people think?"

"People will laugh."

"I may fail."

"I am too busy."

"My family responsibilities will not allow me to do that."

"I'm too old to try that."

"No one else has done that before."

This is "The List" that often comes to mind when we consider pursuing our dream.

The List kills your dream and your vision. If you believe in The List more than in yourself, you are killing your creative power. The Bible says, "Where there is no vision, the people perish" (Proverbs 29:18). Without your creative power, you cannot live your dream; at that point, you are in a condition of death. Working for the realization of your dream or vision gives you a reason to live.

For many of us, our vision is clouded with the obstacles and problems of life; we are blinded by our reasons for not being able to do something and why it will not work. There is no vision; therefore, we have perished, becoming the living dead. A resurrection occurs when we decide to pursue our dream and develop our creative power.

Money is the illusion this world has used to kill many visions. We immediately point to our lack of money as a reason we cannot proceed. Or, we waste time thinking of people or institutions that will give us their money so we can fulfill our vision. Most of the time no one will give us the money that we need. Consequently, we believe we cannot move forward, and our vision dies simply for lack of funding.

Lack of money is not your problem; lack of faith, creativity, and patience is. With faith, creativity, and patience, you will not see money as an obstacle. You will see the vision and draw on your creative powers to make your thoughts a reality. Start small with a creative mind, and what and whom you need will come in time.

Our vision and its realization give us reasons to live, learn, and achieve. Our vision and its realization give us purpose and a mission. Accept your dream, your vision. Do not worry why it will not work. It is your destiny and purpose. Your motion will create opportunities. You must first find a tree and get started.

Do not seek anyone's permission to fulfill your vision. Once you feel in your heart that this is your dream, mission, and purpose, then you have already been given permission. Living your dream will not be easy, so you must want to do it with all your being.

Reflect on your dream. Are you passionate about achieving it? Yes, there are many reasons why your dream may not happen. The odds may well be against you, but if you are prepared to struggle and sacrifice your money, time, mind, and life to live your dream, then move forward. Find a tree and get started.

We were not born to fail. The List cannot defeat you. The List only tests you. Overcoming the obstacles presented by The List is necessary. Through this process, you learn and draw out your creative genius. Once you tap into your creative genius, The List ceases to enter into your consciousness; you begin instinctively to recognize that problems have solutions. As you tap into your creative genius, you are on the road to becoming a creator, a god.

The following are two examples from personal experience that a "sane" person would not have attempted, and with good reason. These examples demonstrate that you never know what can happen unless you try.

In preparing for the International Black MBA Student Association Conference, I wanted the president of Zimbabwe, President Robert Mugabe, to attend as a keynote speaker. Mugabe, who at that time was revered by the world for his leadership, made education his nation's top budgetary priority. Several people told me that they knew people in Zimbabwe who could get an invitation to President Mugabe. After all the contacts came up short, faced with not having the president speak, I decided I had to make an attempt myself.

From a phone booth at UCLA, I contacted the international operator and requested information in Zimbabwe. I asked for the number to the State House, the Zimbabwean equivalent of the White House, and I called the number. Using my most authoritative voice, I identified myself as a caller from the United States trying to reach the president. After several transfers to other operators and staff people at the Zimbabwean State House, I was finally transferred to President Mugabe's personal secretary. I took a deep breath so that my voice would not quiver, and asked to speak to the president.

The phone went silent.

The male secretary reflected on my request. Finally, he said, "This sounds important...the president is at his residence. Would you like that number?" Stunned, I stammered, "Yes. That will be fine."

113

I called President Mugabe's residence.

Again, a series of operators answered. Finally, I recognized the president's distinctive voice from my time spent working in Zimbabwe. "May I help you?" he asked. I closed my eyes, leaned my head against the wall of the phone booth, and started talking. President Mugabe could not attend the conference, but at least I had the opportunity to ask him.

The other personal experience was when I attempted to arrange a meeting with Mrs. Hillary Rodham Clinton for a dignitary who was visiting Los Angeles the same day as Mrs. Clinton.

While studying for the California bar exam, I got a message from this friend, whose husband is well known, but not of the same political affiliation as the Clintons. She asked for discretion in arranging a meeting with Mrs. Clinton. My friend said, "Daniel, Mrs. Clinton is in Los Angeles today. Could you arrange for me to meet her?" I heard myself saying to my friend, "Yes, ma'am, I'll call you in one hour."

How was I ever going to make that happen?

I raced back to the second floor of the library to get my books. As I drove home, The List hit me. Why did I say yes? I did not know anyone in the political world. The security around Mrs. Clinton would be intense. I did not even know where to start on this one!

As I drove, I said a prayer. By the time I got home, I had about thirty minutes to call my friend back with an update. I remembered that the person I worked for at the Democratic National Convention many years earlier now worked for Mrs. Clinton. I called information in Washington, D.C. I called the White House. I tried reaching the person for whom I had worked but could not get through. When I reached a staff assistant in Mrs. Clinton's office, I told her that I had to arrange a meeting with Mrs. Clinton and a VIP, whose name I could not reveal. Before letting her respond, I quickly acknowledged how preposterous my request was, but I gently asked her to work with me. The White House assistant said she would have to call me back. That was a small opening.

I jumped into the shower in case I had to move fast. While showering, the White House returned my call and left a message. I called back. The person at the White House now sounded less willing to work with me, and she shrieked in a voice of disbelief, "You want to arrange a meeting between the First Lady of the United States of America and a VIP, and you cannot tell me this person's name?"

I said matter-of-factly, "Yes."

Seven hours after the initial call, my friend was shaking Mrs. Clinton's hand.

There are many reasons why these attempts should not have worked, but if you use your creative mind and focus on the objective–and not on The List–then the possibilities will open up for you.

CHAPTER 18

Lead Yourself

"People are not really afraid of dying; they're afraid of not ever having lived, not ever having deeply considered their life's higher purpose, and not ever having stepped into that purpose and at least tried to make a difference in this world."

—Joseph Jaworski

To reach your potential and to make a difference, determine your vision of a better world and get started making your vision real—even if at first you are alone.

While working in Zimbabwe, I visited South Africa for a week. This visit was during the time of apartheid, the government-sanctioned system of racial separation and oppression. I wanted to see apartheid firsthand and meet with the people of South Africa.

The apartheid army promised to destroy a mother's home and 500 other homes. When I asked her what she was going to do when the army returned with bulldozers and weapons, she picked up a broken Coke bottle and told me she was going to "fight back."

In South Africa I stayed with a colored (mixed-race) family who wanted to take me to see the tourist sites. However, I made it clear that I wanted to see the Soweto township and meet with representatives of the various political parties in order to gain insight into life under apartheid. A Methodist pastor took me to an area where the army had come the day before and razed residents' homes. I went inside a "home" that remained standing. Despite being constructed with boards and sheets of tin, it was spotlessly clean inside. After seeing the pride this family took in their home despite poverty, I thought to myself, "This says 'dignity.'"

The pastor gathered the residents whose homes had been destroyed. We distributed tents, and he read the government's letter ordering them to leave or the army would come in to forcibly remove them. I asked a mother what she was going to do. She picked up a broken Coke bottle and defiantly said, "We're going to fight back."

Comforting Residents

Reverend Cecil Begbie speaks with residents who received a letter from the apartheid government demanding they abandon their homes. *Johannesburg, South Africa, April 1985*

While in South Africa, I awoke one morning and read on the front page of a national newspaper that students at Columbia University had taken over the administration building in protest against investment in South Africa. Reports were on South African radio and television. I called the Columbia student newspaper collect to inform them that news of what was going on at Columbia was being reported throughout South Africa. Student reporters informed me that the then president of Columbia had advised the students that Nobel Peace Prize winner, Bishop Desmond Tutu, to whom Columbia had given an honorary degree a year earlier, would be against the students' demonstration. I advised the student reporters that I had a meeting scheduled with Bishop Tutu later that day, and I would ask him where he stood on the issue. He told me that he supported the students and would give words of support that evening when he did a radio interview that would broadcast in New York City.

South Africans told me that the students' actions were an inspiration to them.

Nobel Peace Prize winner Bishop **Desmond Tutu** and I discussed apartheid and the divestment movement at Columbia University.
Johannesburg, South Africa, April 1985

Reflecting back, taking a stand against racism and apartheid appears to have been a natural position to take. At the time, however, our stance and demands were controversial and met with opposition.

Find an issue or problem. Envision a solution. Take action in bringing about a solution and a change.

LEADERSHIP

In the fall of 1995 I was hired to organize the Los Angeles leg of a United States tour by the then president of the Republic of Ghana, Jerry Rawlings. During his stay, the president and members of his delegation were invited to attend the "Soul Train Award," an annual event to honor black musical artists. The president's entourage arrived at the Shrine Auditorium after the taping of the program had begun. Rapper Tupac Shakur, Magic Johnson, Whitney Houston, and Stevie Wonder were all there. The president and first lady sat in the first row. Seated next to them and directly behind President and Mrs. Rawlings were security agents from the United States and Ghana. Members of the president's delegation sat behind him. I stood off the main floor, attentive to any need a member of the delegation might have. At a break during the show's taping, a secret service agent sitting next to President Rawlings motioned for me to come over and sit there. As I sat next to the President and Mrs. Rawlings surrounded by Hollywood's elite, I asked myself, "Should I talk to the president during the next break in the taping?" As I debated with myself, I finally resolved my dilemma by asking myself, "What would Lucy do?" Having been a lifelong fan of the television program, *I Love Lucy*, I concluded that Lucy would talk to the president. Having observed President Rawlings for two days, I wondered how he really knew what was going on around him and in his country when everyone approached him with such deference and adoration. I asked, "Mr. President, how do you really know what is going on when everyone comes to you in their 'Sunday best?'" President Rawlings proceeded to explain to me that he and the first lady do not sit in the Castle, the Ghanaian equivalent of the White House, and receive reports. He and his wife go out to the villages and cities and meet with citizens to see what is going on for themselves firsthand. As we continued our conversation during subsequent breaks, a secret service agent sitting in the seat behind me poked me in the back and whispered that I should leave the president alone, but President Rawlings tapped me on the knee to continue our dialogue as I shared with him my experiences of working with the youth in his country. As the president engaged me at each break and the agent repeatedly requested that I be quiet, I felt like Lucy—caught in a predicament again.

His Excellency, The President

I organized **President Rawlings'** visit to Los Angeles and he encouraged me to return to Ghana. *Beverly Hills, California, November 1, 1995* (Photo by Howard Bingham)

Leaders must get out and do the dirty work. People respond to leaders who do. That lesson I learned from President Rawlings. Leaders must have a vision and take action. Then they involve others to help make the vision a reality.

121

President Rawlings received my mother and family members at his official residence: the Castle. Following our meeting, the president flew us in his helicopter to his retreat for dinner. *Accra, Ghana, March 6, 1998*

Leadership

Jerry Rawlings, then president of Ghana, cleans the sewer to prevent the spread of malaria. *Accra, Ghana, 1997*

You can make a difference.

Find a tree and get started.

Your seemingly insignificant local actions
can have an international impact.

They Found Their Tree
Soul 2 Sole: International Bridge of Goodwill

by Lauren Dorsey

I first heard of Daniel Armstrong and the Find A Tree program at the Young Black Scholars kick off during my freshman year at Chadwick School. The things Daniel said motivated me, but I was not taking notes or listening as carefully as I should have. I was fortunate to experience a second encounter with him at my junior class retreat where my classmates and I participated in a hands-on workshop focused on finding our dreams. That session had a greater impact on me because we discussed in small groups what our dreams were and we actually wrote them down. This is what helped me to get started: writing my goals down. That was the day I decided that I was going to create "Soul 2 Sole," which is a shoe drive I conceived, aimed to help the disadvantaged living in South Africa's poorest communities heal from the oppressiveness of apartheid. I had been thinking about this idea previously and was actually inspired to do it while reading a book called *Kaffir Boy*, a memoir by Mark Mathabane about his experience growing up under apartheid. In *Kaffir Boy*, I distinctly remembered Mathabane's description of sleeping on cardboard-padded floors night after night while rats and vicious ants gnawed at his feet and those of his younger siblings to the point where they were unable to walk for days. As this gruesome image played continuously in my mind, I began to feel compassion for South Africa's destitute. Reading that made me say, "Wow! How privileged and blessed I am." I looked in my closet, saw several pairs of shoes and realized these children have nothing. From there I went step-by-step following the Find A Tree program. I wrote my goals down and gave myself deadlines.

Some I completed, and some I did not. I went back to school and started my project the second semester. I chose to share the project with the Chadwick School student body, and I kicked off Soul 2 Sole. I created the name, Soul 2 Sole, because I believed it best illustrated souls at home caring for sole-less feet abroad. My ultimate goal was to collect 1,000 pairs of shoes, and the catchy name helped attract my peers and encouraged them to get involved. I collected the shoes in the library, and the piles of shoes served as a daily reminder for other students and teachers to give. Soon there were mounds of shoes, and the librarian begged me to relocate the shoes because they were starting to release an overwhelming odor. About fifteen upper school students helped me organize and relocate the shoes to the athletic department's storage area. I found that many of my classmates were willing to donate their shoes, but when it came time to do the actual labor, not many were willing to cooperate. I was very grateful for those who did.

After we had the shoes organized in storage, I started writing letters to companies asking them to support the project by financing the delivery. Compaq Computer Corporation agreed to support Soul 2 Sole by paying for the shipping and packaging fees. The excitement of collecting so many pairs of shoes and receiving the corporate sponsorship was such a tremendous accomplishment that I reluctantly failed to research how exactly I was going to get the shoes to South Africa. I was unaware of the South African import regulations that required a humanitarian verification permit before donations could enter the country. I completed the permit application and necessary paperwork, but my attempts to acquire the necessary permit were unrecognized. I still had not received a response or even a reply that stated that my request has been received and awaited assessment. After time went by, I realized that I either needed someone in South Africa to walk my application through the system, or work resourcefully to adjust my approach to get the children their shoes.

Mr. Armstrong helped me to locate Mrs. Jacqui Ahrends, the community service coordinator at St. Cyprian, an all-girls school in Cape Town, South Africa. Jacqui and I communicated through email and occasional conference calls and discussed the economic roadblocks and South African importing regulations that hindered Soul 2 Sole's progress. After further research I later discovered that used textiles sent to South Africa from America and Europe were actually disrupting South Africa's textile industry and thus its economy. In the end, Soul 2 Sole exported the originally collected shoes to flood victims in Accra, Ghana, through a program called Soul-Save International. We were also able to use the promised support and money from Compaq Computer Corporation to buy new shoes from South African merchandisers for the orphans living in Sakhumzi Children's Home in Cape Town. Jacqui had shared with me previously that shoes were considered gold in most South African townships, and the thought of "new" shoes was absolutely unconceivable. I have beautiful pictures of the kids getting new shoes and an article that appeared in the South African press.

Completing Soul 2 Sole was the most exhilarating moment of my high school experience. I felt very accomplished that my passion and persistence prevailed over the obstacles that repeatedly threatened the project's progress. I learned that by acknowledging the problem and finding a small way to comfort those suffering, I can have a greater impact than imaginable, for I found that not only did Soul 2 Sole help the people of South Africa and Ghana, but it also encouraged my peers and people in my community to develop a similar compassion for others. Like a snowball effect, blessings after blessings have continued, and I feel that I have truly made a difference.

Jacqui Ahrends, the community service coordinator at St. Cyprian in Cape Town, South Africa, wrote of Lauren's accomplishment:

"Congratulations, [Lauren] on your extraordinary work with Soul 2 Sole. We are humbled by your compassion, enchanted by your courage, and awestruck by your tenacity as you work toward putting shoes on children from materially underprivileged communities! It has been wonderful to work with you and to have had the privilege of purchasing the shoes for Sakhumzi's children, sharing in their delight too. It is role models like you, Lauren, who are an inspiration to us all. Keep up the outstanding work and we look forward to hosting you in South Africa one day soon!"

CHAPTER 19

Start a Business

"Google's first 'international headquarters' was a garage."
—Larry Page, Google co-founder

Apple Computers began in a garage.

Amazon.com began in a garage.

Facebook began in a dorm room.

MONEY

Money is a by-product of excellence. Focus on excellence, and then on how to receive a value for your service or product. Once you have mastered your skill or talent, then you can begin to turn your gift into a business. Customers will come to you and give you money not because your rent is due, but because you can offer them excellence in the form of the product or service. Produce excellence. Customers and money will follow.

Basketball superstar, Michael Jordan, and technology mastermind, Steve Jobs, were driven to achieve and perfect their vision and dreams. The level of excellence that they achieved produced their wealth. They did not perfect their product and develop their talent driven by dreams of money or new cars. They had clear thoughts and images in their minds of what they wanted to be, do, and achieve. They were driven to make the images in their minds real in their pursuit of excellence.

We all want to be rich, although for many people winning the lottery seems to be the only way. The most direct route to wealth is to have your own business. You do not have to invent something the world has never seen before to become wealthy. Get into motion developing, learning, and perfecting your gifts. Produce excellence and develop a business around your talents. As the song says, "God bless the child that's got his own." Your God can only bring you money-making opportunities (i.e., customers) when you are in motion. Then He can truly bless you with the wealth of the world. With a business, you are ready to receive His blessings in the form of business opportunities.

Wealth is waiting for you. Be in a position to receive wealth by being in business.

YOUR BUSINESS

Your business can be based on your individual talents and gifts.

Begin part time. Build understanding and gradually structure your service as a business. As you produce excellence, your part-time hobby can evolve into your full-time job.

Because this activity is the one you have chosen and love to do, once it becomes a business, it will not feel like work. You will then be making money doing what you enjoy. This passion and love will motivate you to work when all others are ready to go home.

Although I "retired" from playing basketball after my junior year in college, I still had the skills to create a business and a job for myself teaching basketball.

While studying for the bar exam, I began giving private basketball lessons. Once again, I was in the gym with a ball and my music. My job now was to let someone else come inside my basketball heaven with me. I turned my skill, basketball, into a business. I called my service To Be a Champion. My job was to listen to music and play basketball. The one-on-one tutorials grew in popularity, and each month new players wanted to join me in my office, the gym.

A parent of one player said, "I'll pay you $10,000 for a month of lessons, and if that is not enough, I'll pay more." This parent had already given me a Jeep when my car had broken down, so I knew I could believe him. Unfortunately, the parent wanted the lessons more than the son did.

After seeing one session, the coach of a professional team from South Korea hired me to train his team. This team paid me well to do what I love.

CUSTOMER BASE: THE FOUNDATION OF AN ENTERPRISE

Successful businesses will often provide the basic services and goods that we need regularly, such as lawn mowing, dry cleaning, and providing food. When starting your business, the mundane is often the most reliable. You do not have to invent a new computer chip to start a business.

One strategy to build a customer base is to develop your talent into a service and volunteer. If you are good at what you do, word will spread, and soon someone will ask if he can pay you for what you previously had done for free.

Mastery of human relations is critical for business success. Poor human relations impede the development of many businesses. Effective human relations skills will aid in establishing a customer base, the business's foundation.

To win customers and to maintain a customer base are challenges of all businesses. One must learn how to serve. Serving the customer takes humility and mastery of human relations. The successful business goes the extra mile to serve and to satisfy the customer. Through proper conduct, a business can build its customers' trust and confidence. This trust and confidence will be critical in getting referrals and when offering additional services or products to current customers. Treat your customers well, and they will refer you to their friends.

BUILDING YOUR BUSINESS

Prepare your business plan. There are software applications specially designed to walk you through the steps of preparing a business plan. Here are a few essential elements:

1. Product or Service

Describe your product or service. Why should someone buy from you? List the benefits of your product or service. Why would a customer do business with you rather than with a competitor?

2. Marketing

Marketing is everything you do, not just the end product or service. How do you answer the phone? What is the quality of the paper you use for stationery? Are you on time? How do you dress? We send messages about who we are in everything we do. Customers are watching. Commit yourself to your best in all that you do, and customers will want to do business with you.

INITIAL CUSTOMERS: START WITH FRIENDS AND FAMILY

Those who love us should be most willing to take a chance on our new venture. Do not take the business of family or friends for granted. When working on a business matter with them, be professional, even it feels strange to be "professional" with someone you know so well. They may love you as a family member or friend, but may not refer you unless they are confident you can do the job that you advertise.

Advertising is usually necessary, but referrals are better. The strongest businesses have a loyal customer base. Not only do customers come back, but they will provide free advertising to their friends and family members.

To ensure a loyal customer base, commit yourself to quality. If you are more demanding and meticulous than the customer, they should have nothing to complain about. Someone will eventually find fault, but with effective human relations skills and a demonstrated commitment to customer satisfaction, a complaining customer can be transformed into an advocate for your business.

Customers are buying you first and the product or service second. If you are bored with your business and what it has to offer, why should customers be interested? Enthusiasm is the magic that brings people to life. If you are enthusiastic, then your customers will take notice and listen to your pitch.

Advertising does not have to be expensive. Be creative. Use social media. Knock on doors. Leave your business card with everyone you meet. The best advertisement is a happy customer. Make them happy, and word will spread. Produce excellence, and money will follow.

SELLING

If a potential customer has a legitimate need for your product or service, and has said "no" to your invitation to do business, remember: "no" means "maybe." You must identify the obstacle that is stopping the transaction and then figure out how to go from "no" to "yes." One afternoon during the time I operated my company, Dirt Patrol Cleaning Service, I was $300 short of making payroll, which was due the next day. Late in the afternoon, I got a call for a "Dirt Alert" (a dirty carpet). I told the lady we would be right over. My "partners in grime" rushed through the streets to get to the grime scene. I knew the area, and all the homes were large, so I was confident that once I got inside I would detect $300 worth of grime. Once inside, the "grime scene" (the carpet) was a mess. I beamed with enthusiasm, "I will be able to make payroll after all!" I thought. After measuring the carpet to be cleaned, the estimate came to $335. The homeowner looked at me and emphatically said, "No." I remembered that "no" means "maybe." Determined to turn her away from a "life of grime," I asked, "What will it take for us to clean her house?" She said, "My budget is $300 and not a penny more." I said fine. The "grime fighters" went to work arresting dirt and fighting grime. We were paid the $300, and I was able to meet payroll. I identified the obstacle, $35, and offered a solution, a $35 discount. "No" means "maybe." Find the obstacle and overcome it.

CUSTOMER FOLLOW UP

Whenever appropriate, follow up with your customers. Your job is to make sure they are happy. If they are not totally satisfied with your product or service, find out why and correct it. If they are satisfied, thank them. Regardless of their response, you will collect valuable information and lay the foundation for a long-term business relationship.

3. Budget

List what you need to get started and to operate for six months.

Now figure out how to start without all you listed above.

Musician Herb Alpert and partner Jerry Moss started A&M Records in Alpert's garage. The company that launched the careers of Janet Jackson, Sting, and the Police eventually sold for approximately a half billion dollars. The computer company Hewlett-Packard also started in a garage. Wally "Famous" Amos baked chocolate chip cookies at home and gave them to friends as gifts. His charity grew into the Famous Amos Cookie Company, a multimillion-dollar firm.

Find a tree and get started!
Your business can be doing what you love.
Produce excellence and start a business.

They Found Their Tree
Scoring Points with NBA Executives

by Matthew Fournier

The first time I heard Daniel Armstrong speak was when he came to my high school, Chadwick. He spoke about Find A Tree. This meeting gave me the idea of creating a basketball scouting service and sending out my basketball report to professional teams. I love to watch college games and analyze players' strengths and weaknesses. I first met Jim Paxton, the general manager of the Cleveland Cavaliers basketball team, about three or four years ago. At that time he asked me to start writing scouting reports of prospective professional players and send them to him. However, I did not take the idea seriously. Then I heard Daniel speak at a conference, and he caused me to think that my idea could one day become an actual business. As I thought about it, I realized that I could succeed and develop a scouting service or work in sports management as a career after college. Pursuing my dream started a whole new path for me. I began thinking about the concept, my thoughts began to grow, and it came together. I came out with a detailed scouting report on college basketball players. I sent my report to the Cleveland team. They were so impressed that they sent it on to the Chicago Bulls.

For my scouting service I watched college basketball games, focusing on prospective professional players. I analyzed the players' strengths and weaknesses on both offense and defense. I also shared my view on which players would be able to play at the professional level. Currently, I am sending my report to Chicago, Cleveland, Sacramento, and next season to Los Angeles.

My scouting service grew from something that was just for fun to a business, and it has been growing each season by one or two teams who request to receive my scouting reports and analyses. Now I am thinking about becoming a general manager ten to twenty years down the line. Maybe I will intern during college to see how things are run and then after college work as a scout or assistant general manager and eventually become a general manager, where I will be making trades and drafting players. Find A Tree helped me to understand that I can become a general manager and achieve my dream. Find A Tree continues to show me how to work toward my dream and become better and more successful.

MATTHEW FOURNIER UPDATE

From 2008 to 2012, Mathew worked at J.P. Morgan Securities where he helped manage over $1 billion in assets. Matthew is currently studying at Columbia University, where he's obtaining his MBA.

Mathew writes of his experience with Find A Tree:

"Daniel taught me early on that passion is the key to living a happy and meaningful life. A life where one's personal actions make him or her happy, but also a life that has a positive impact on the world is the goal. He also taught me that passion is transferable; by finding a passion in one thing, over time, it can transfer to other interests. One just has to find a tree and get started.

"My first passion was basketball. From the age of thirteen and throughout my teenage years—with Daniel's help—I took that passion and energy and became a part-time NBA scout for a number of teams, including the Cleveland Cavaliers. It was a great job that made me

happy and kept me out of trouble, while also guiding me down the path toward college. Then, in college, I discovered my next passion: finance and economics. Again, using the tools and lessons Daniel taught me at an early age, I have used my energy and passion to help start companies, non-profits, and manage significant amounts of money at J.P. Morgan. As I mature and learn, I have realized that Daniel was and is right: passion—finding your tree and getting started—is the key to life. Thank you for your help, Daniel. I could not have made it without your guidance."

- Matthew Fournier

Los Angeles, California

CHAPTER 20

Work in Harmony with Universal Law (There Is No Santa Claus)

"There is no easy walk to freedom anywhere, and many of us will have to pass through the valley of the shadow of death again and again before we reach the mountain top of our desires."
—Nelson Mandela

"After one has discovered what he is called for, he should set out to do it with all of the power that he has in his system. Do it as if God almighty ordained you at this particular moment in history to do it."
—Martin Luther King, Jr.

THE LAW OF MOTION

If there is no force acting on a body, it will continue in its state of rest. Objects in motion tend to stay in motion.

"Inertia"—that which opposes a body from making any change in its current state.

Unless you get up and do something to move your dream from a thought to reality, your dream will not manifest. You must force yourself to do something—anything. Just start. Santa Claus is not going to bring you your dream. Hoping, wishing, and waiting will not make your dream a reality. You must use your desire for the dream as energy to create motion. Even if the starting point is merely thinking about your interests and talents and just thinking about how you can serve humanity, these thoughts are the initial stages of motion. Things in motion tend to stay in motion. Follow these thoughts with doing research and writing a plan. Make the first step or first phase of your plan so simple that it will be easy to complete. Do something. Overcome the inertia—that which is stopping you from proceeding. Our thoughts create the strongest inertia. We tell ourselves why we should and must continue to do nothing. Another source of inertia is the belief that we lack resources. Your motion, your desire, and your energy will overcome this perceived obstacle as well.

YOU ARE RICH IN RESOURCES

When you take action and don't allow The List to stop you, the universe is your resource base. Events and people begin coming to you once you are in motion.

Many people use their faith in their God or Supreme Being as a connection to the universe of resources. Others feel that coincidence or luck is their connection to the universe. Your God or your connection will help you by bringing you what you need when you need it. (You may disagree with your God as to what you need and just how quickly you want it, but your God knows best when you are ready.)

To utilize the universal resource, we must be in harmony with universal law. Motion is essential for life. Water that stays in motion gives life. Water that is stagnant for a period of time becomes a poison. Living your dream puts you in motion. Fulfilling those dreams gives your life meaning, purpose, fulfillment, and abundance. However, if we become stationary, we become like a poison to ourselves and to those around us.

Universal law, your God, or good luck does not work like Santa Claus. Your God is not going to give you what you desire like a gift from St. Nick. As children, we were raised to believe in Santa Claus. We grew up thinking and expecting our wishes to be granted by God the same way that we expected gifts from Santa. Get in motion first, and that motion will eventually bring you the resources and knowledge that you need.

Having money and access to resources is not a guarantee that one will be on the path to pursuing dreams. Having a dream backed by a strong desire and action can be more valuable an asset than money.

There Is No Santa Claus

Students from Chadwick, an exclusive private school, visited the Find A Tree students at Nelles Youth Correctional Facility with the intention of helping the juvenile inmates turn their lives around. The Chadwick students left the meeting realizing that despite their education and economic advantages, no one was going to give them their dream. They too needed to find their tree and get started. *Whittier, California, April 29, 2000*

In February of 2000 I was invited to facilitate a workshop for the eleventh grade class at Chadwick School, a private school whose tuition is over $30,000 a year. Many students shared their dream to help solve society's problems—homelessness, hunger, poverty, etc. I advised them that they might need to leave the comforts of Palos Verdes and come down and visit students in the Find A Tree program who were incarcerated at the California Youth Authority's Fred C. Nelles facility. A delegation of Chadwick students agreed to meet with young men incarcerated at Nelles. As we drove to the facility, the students seemed concerned about entering a jail, but were eager to advise and help the young juvenile offenders to turn their lives around. During the discussion with the inmates, who had just completed a seven-month Find A Tree course, the moderator asked the group what they were doing in their own community to build a better world. The young men from the juvenile jail explained how they were pursuing their dreams despite being locked up. One was working toward owning his own construction company and had been reading and working with a mentor from Habitat for Humanity, the non-profit organization that builds low-cost housing. Another shared how he had organized a class on auto mechanics for himself and other inmates not in the Find A Tree program. Another had begun a school on his unit. When it came time for the Chadwick students to share, they were silent. The group waited for a volunteer. Still silence. Finally, a Chadwick student hesitantly raised her hand, slightly embarrassed, and said, "You guys here are better than us. We have everything in Palos Verdes, but we're not doing anything with it." A young man from the facility responded by saying, "We're not better. We have simply found our tree and gotten started. You just need to go back to Palos Verdes and do the same."

Stunned, the Chadwick students left the correctional facility recognizing that they went there to help, but they got helped instead. Despite all of their resources, with no dream and creative mind to find their tree, they were doing less than young men with little education and no resources. These young men in jail, who were challenging their conditions and working to change their futures, are prime examples of the power of not waiting. They dreamed, found a tree, and got started.

No one respects a beggar, complainer, or one who gives excuses. Your God is the Creator—the Builder. To be in sync with Him and to fully operate in accord with Him, we need to be like Him. We must become creators and builders, not beggars and complainers. ("Oh, God, I need rent money." "Oh, God, please help me get that new car.") If you need money, start a business. Then your God can bring business opportunities that provide the money you would like to have. You must first get started, and not expect a gift. Once you get started, then opportunities, thoughts, and people will come to help.

You must become a builder and a creator.

Then the resources of the universe will begin to come to you.

Have faith and take action.

Once you are in motion, you create circumstances and opportunities that you did not realize awaited you. You may move into dimensions and worlds you never dreamed possible.

Each step leads to the next opportunity.

Put service to others first. Give of your talents, and the world will open up to you.

Never give credence to the things that you believe will prevent you from becoming successful.

Just find a tree and get started.

CHAPTER 21

Where Do We Go from Here?

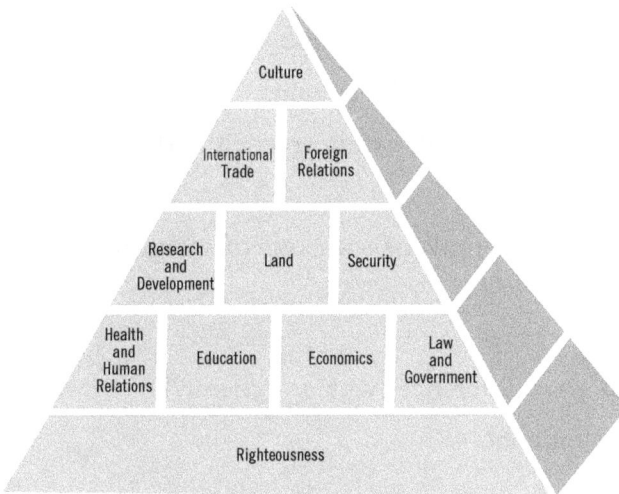

WHAT YOU CAN DO

Just as builders follow blueprints, the Building a Better World Pyramid is your blueprint for building a better world. A blueprint is a program of action. The reader (yes, you, holding this book or tablet) must now decide first where you fit in the Pyramid. Second, determine what you are going to do to make that block or blocks a reality, and find a tree and get started.

When you find your tree and get started, you will bring meaning and purpose to your life, you will make a difference, and you will help to build a better world.

RIGHTEOUSNESS

- Keep your word.
- Listen to your conscience.
- Lower your voice.
- Pray.
- Read the Bible, Quran, Torah, or the book that inspires you.
- Fast.
- Give money and/or time to a charity.
- Give food to a homeless person.
- Say "I love you" to a loved one.
- Acknowledge a fault within yourself and work to improve it.
- Gossip less.
- Follow the example of someone of integrity whom you admire.
- Listen to others.
- Settle your differences with an "enemy."
- Help someone.

HEALTH AND HUMAN RELATIONS

- Eat less junk food.
- Make peace with someone with whom you have had differences in the past.
- Practice courtesy.
- Smoke less.
- Make a list of twenty characteristics that you like about yourself.
- List five characteristics about yourself that you would like to improve.

- Contact a loved one or friend and tell him or her what you admire about that person.

- Eliminate one unhealthy item from your diet.

- Exercise a little bit more today than you did yesterday.

- List twenty interests, talents, and gifts that you have.

- Determine a dream.

- Read *How to Live Your Dreams: Find a Tree and Get Started*.

- Read *How to Win Friends & Influence People* by Dale Carnegie.

- Invite friends over and let each guest share his or her life story.

- Invite friends over to share their dreams.

- Help your friends to realize their dreams.

EDUCATION

- Read a book on a subject you would like to learn more about.

- Improve your grades.

- Form a book club.

- Read a newspaper or magazine regularly.

- Start a Saturday school in your home.

- Take a class.

- Make of list of ten subjects about which you would like to learn more.

- Meet with your child's teacher.

- Join a local P.T.A.

- Write a plan to improve your school.

- Compliment an outstanding teacher.

- Start a charter school.

- Return to school.

- Teach someone.
- Volunteer in a school.

ECONOMICS

- Identify your talents and determine which are marketable as a service.
- Make something and sell it.
- Read the business section of the newspaper.
- Form a neighborhood food co-operative.
- Start a business.
- Bake cookies and sell them.
- Dream of a business you would like to own one day.
- Read about starting a business.
- Support a small business.
- Make a flyer promoting your business.
- Produce excellence in your business.
- Provide your customers with better service today than you did yesterday.
- Form a business incubator with your friends.
- Pool your resources with your friends to advance each other's business.

LAW AND GOVERNMENT

- Register to vote.
- Vote.
- Work in a campaign.
- Run for office.

- Organize a neighborhood dispute resolution center.

- Attend law school.

- Serve on a jury.

- Settle your differences with an adversary.

- Identify a leader or organization that you support and volunteer.

- Discuss with family members what each member's expectations and responsibilities to the family are and write down how each will contribute.

- Organize a peace summit with local youth.

- Teach youth in your community the Find A Tree principles.

- Help youth to determine and pursue their dreams.

- Create a code of behavior within your neighborhood to build a stronger community.

- Identify principles of life that inspire you and work to uphold them in your life.

SECURITY

- Take a self-defense class.

- Get an emergency supplies kit.

- Talk to your children about safety.

- Form a Neighborhood Watch program.

- Meet your neighbors.

- Install dead-bolt locks.

- Install smoke detectors.

- Learn CPR.

- Work with the youth in your neighborhood and determine their interests and dreams.

- Help young people realize their dreams.

- Set up athletic leagues in your neighborhood.
- Serve as a mentor for a young person.
- Help someone fighting drug addiction.
- Help someone find a job.
- Build your community by working together to organize a neighborhood party.

LAND

- Recycle your home garbage.
- Plant a garden.
- Pick up some trash.
- Take the bus.
- Water your plants.
- Plant a tree.
- Learn the location of the countries of the world.
- Study water retrieval and purification.
- Study land cultivation.
- Study soil fertilization.
- Take a class in geology.
- Buy an electric car.
- Install solar panels in your home.
- Buy organic food.
- Organize a neighborhood cleanup and beautification project.

RESEARCH AND DEVELOPMENT

- Study your life and your interests.
- List your interests, talents, and gifts and determine a dream.

- Get books related to your dream and read them.

- Write a plan of action on realizing your dream.

- Identify and meet individuals experienced in an area related to your dream.

- Reflect on the obstacles that you may face in pursuing your dream.

- Develop strategies to overcome the obstacles that you may face to actualize your dream.

- Identify a community, national, or world problem and research current strategies to address these issues.

- Research and develop your own strategies to address the community, national, or world issue that interests you.

- Apply your proposed solution to that problem in your own community.

- Create a life plan.

- Create goals for the next five years of your life.

- Create monthly goals for the next year.

- Determine weekly and daily priorities to meet the monthly goals.

- Prepare and implement a time management schedule to accomplish all of your daily priorities.

FOREIGN RELATIONS

- Ask someone from another country for a contact who can serve as your pen pal.

- Read about a foreign country and its people.

- Read a history book about a country in the news.

- Study a foreign language.

- Study a culture other than your own.

- Eat at a restaurant with food from another country that is unfamiliar to you.

- Use the Internet to meet people in foreign nations.

- Speak at a school about your travels to a foreign nation.

- When traveling abroad, collect letters from a local school and deliver them to students abroad.

- Invite people from different parts of the world to your home for an international potluck dinner.

- Invite dinner guests to share their nations' customs and history.

- Form a group that travels abroad with a group discount.

- Interact with local people when traveling abroad.

- Join the Peace Corps.

- Take a semester abroad.

INTERNATIONAL TRADE

- Identify the products in your home that are produced in another country.

- Read a book on international trade.

- Discuss the economic needs of a foreign country with an international pen pal.

- Research the economic needs of foreign nation.

- Write to the trade officer of a foreign nation's embassy or consulate and get information on that country.

- Speak with a foreign nation's trade officer about the needs of his or her country.

- Travel to a foreign nation to identify business possibilities.

- Identify organizations whose members are foreign nationals.

- Share your interest in exploring business opportunities with foreign nationals.

- Discuss with international businesspeople their experiences.
- Use the Internet to get information on a foreign nation's economic development and trade requirements.
- Study the impact of globalization on economic development.
- Study the impact and effectiveness of the World Bank and IMF programs.
- Establish a trade relationship with a friend in another country based on barter.

CULTURE

- Clean your house.
- Paint a picture.
- Take an art class.
- Visit a museum.
- Go to an art showing.
- Read a book on etiquette.
- Go to a play.
- Write a poem.
- Organize a talent show.
- Go to a concert.
- Curse less.
- Write the lessons of your life and the wisdom you have gained.
- Invite your friends to write the lessons of their lives and the wisdom they have learned. Share information with each other.
- Pray for knowledge, wisdom, and understanding.

CHAPTER 22

Conclusion: Building a Better World

ACHIEVING YOUR DREAM

We are all born with the creative power to enable us to live our dreams. No one can give it to you, deny you, or give you permission to live your dreams. Once you recognize and tap into your creative power, there is no need to beg, complain, or wait for someone else. In addition to achieving our personal dreams and vision, we must build solutions to our communities' and the world's problems.

The road may not be straight or smooth, but challenging your creative powers will advance your evolution to reaching your potential. Once you are in the motion of living your dream, you will see events and circumstances work in harmony with you. Events and people working in accordance with your God will come to help you overcome obstacles and achieve. This motion will give you the confidence and faith to implement your vision and to reach for more. You then become empowered. You are on the path toward becoming a creator.

Your motion, success, and energy will impact those who are not living their dreams. Others who had discounted their dreams will recognize through your example that people can live their dreams. Your motion will awaken the creative energy of those around you to live their dream as well.

The greatest people in history made positive contributions through serving others and living for something greater than themselves. As we dream, plan, study, and develop a vision beyond our personal well-being, we are advancing and refining our own creative powers and evolving into one with the Creator.

Dreams of personal success, independence, and a comfortable lifestyle are not the final destination. Our dreams and imagination must expand to ways we can serve humanity. We cease our evolution toward fulfilling our full powers as human beings if we limit our dreams to our own well-being and success. A baby is concerned only with himself or herself and demands through its crying the attention of parents. However, with maturity a child is taught to give and share in order to develop and succeed. As adults, if we focus exclusively on our personal well-being, we remain infants in the realization of our full potential. Grow from a "me" focus to "we."

The challenges and obstacles of solving society's problems are great. A champion in sport is tested, developed, and proven as a result of opposition. To become champions as human beings we must take on the challenges of our time. The challenge of implementing your dream for humanity and the struggle this challenge involves will advance your evolutionary development, refine your power as a creator, and ultimately move you closer to being in harmony with your God.

All our dreams are interconnected. As you give to the broader community, resources and people come to you to enable you to advance your personal dream. As Native American traditions teach: we are all connected in a circle. This circle of life will bring you rewards and true happiness, and you will receive all that you need to live your dream and fulfill your purpose.

How can you make a better world?

BUILDING A BETTER WORLD

A world of peace begins with each of us connecting and empowering ourselves to live our dream. Our dreams are interconnected. A world of peace will come when we recognize our own power and share our gifts. We will then see value in ourselves and in others regardless of physical packaging. We will be valued for what we are and our contributions rather than for what we have. However, if you're not manifesting your gifts, others will judge you by superficial standards. When we all manifest, share, and connect our talents and dreams, we will build respect, unity, and cooperation. Each member of society must dream and be equipped with an education to manifest one's gifts. Without this action, society will remain fragmented. Segments of people will remain frustrated and dissatisfied, while others who have tapped into their creative powers will live their dream, empowered and reaping the material and psychological benefits.

A world based on peace and righteousness is not going to float down to Earth like magic. We must get in motion to make it happen. This world's present governments and political powers will not legislate a new world based on truth, justice, equality, and righteousness. We must build it. We were all born with the power.

A better world is possible.

Find a tree, and get started.

The Find A Tree Workbook

YOUR ROAD MAP TO TURNING YOUR DREAMS INTO REALITY

PURPOSE

Living your dream can begin once you decide to get into motion.

This workbook will assist you in identifying your dream and then developing a plan of action that will set you in motion toward the realization of your dream and life purpose.

Your mind is your greatest asset. You must use your mind to think and develop a thorough plan of action, which will allow you to put your thoughts and ideas into motion.

The creative process begins with thought, which can then be transformed into reality. *The Find a Tree Workbook* will launch the process of living your dream.

Let's find a tree and get started.

THE SEED

Finding Your Tree

YOUR STORY

Father

Father's name:

Occupation:

Education:

Describe your father's family:

Lessons and values learned from your father:

Briefly describe your father's background:

Describe your father's interests:

Tell what you admire most about your father:

Mother

Mother's name:

Occupation:

Education:

Describe your mother's family:

Lessons and values learned from your mother:

Briefly describe your mother's background:

Describe your mother's interests:

Tell what you admire most about your mother:

Grandfathers

Grandfather's name:

Occupation:

Education:

Describe your grandfather's family:

Lessons and values learned from your grandfather:

Briefly describe your grandfather's background:

Describe your grandfather's interests:

Tell what you admire most about your grandfather:

Grandmothers

Grandmother's name:

Occupation:

Education:

Describe your grandmother's family:

Lessons and values learned from your grandmother:

Briefly describe your grandmother's background:

Describe your grandmother's interests:

Tell what you admire most about your grandmother:

Uncles

Uncle's name:

Occupation:

Education:

Describe your uncle's family:

Lessons and values learned from your uncle:

Briefly describe your uncle's background:

Describe your uncle's interests:

Tell what you admire most about your uncle:

Aunts

Aunt's name:

Occupation:

Education:

Describe your aunt's family:

Lessons and values learned from your aunt:

Briefly describe your aunt's background:

Describe your aunt's interests:

Tell what you admire most about your aunt:

Siblings

List the name(s) of your brothers and sisters and your age difference (for example: John, 2 years older):

Describe your siblings' interests and talents:

Lessons and values learned from each of your siblings:

List qualities you admire about each of your siblings:

DESCRIBE YOURSELF

Your birth date:

Where you were born:

Cities where you lived while growing up:

Activities you enjoyed as a child:

When you were a child, what were your life's ambitions?

Did you ever feel that you were destined to do something in particular?

If yes, what was it that you felt you were destined to do?

Do you still feel you are destined to do that?

If no, why not?

If yes, how are you fulfilling that destiny?

Who encouraged you or was a positive influence on you as a child?

How did that person(s) influence you?

What three words would you use to describe yourself?

1. _____

2. _____

3. _____

List ten key events in your life:

1. _____

2. _____

3. _____

4. _____

5. _____

6. _____

7. _____

8. _____

9. _____

10. _____

Describe how those events have impacted your life.

Make a timeline of your life:

Example:

1985	1990	1994	2003	2011
Born	Dog died	Science fair award	High school graduation	Met best friend

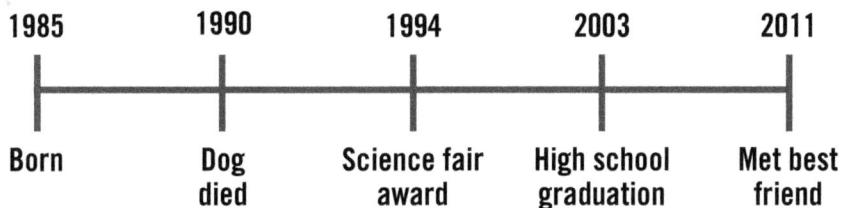

What would you like to improve about yourself?

What can you do to make that change?

How do you spend your free time?

What TV shows do you watch?

What organizations or clubs do you belong to?

What books and magazines do you read?

What were your aspirations while you were in high school?

TALENTS AND INTERESTS

List 20 talents and/or interests that you have:

_____

_____

_____

_____

_____

_____

_____

_____

_____

_____

Did you uncover 20?

If not, keep digging for 20 talents and/or interests.

What makes you unique?

Please complete the following sentences:

I am happiest when I am…

Activities that I love to do are…

Activities that I am naturally good at are…

Activities that I would like to master are…

Life would be so exciting if…

Five achievements that I am most proud of are…

1. _____

2. _____

3. _____

4. _____

5. _____

What bores you?

What frustrates you?

What are you passionate about?

What is important to you?

If you won $100 million in the lottery but had to do something constructive in order to receive the money, how would you spend your time?

My dream job would be to...

Why have you not achieved goals in the past?

In 1 year I hope to...

In 3 years I hope to...

In 5 years I hope to...

What can you begin doing today to realize these projections?

To achieve what I would ideally like to be doing in 1 year, I must begin...

To achieve what I would ideally like to be doing in 3 years, I must begin...

To achieve what I would ideally like to be doing in 5 years, I must begin...

For example, if you listed a monetary goal, what business would you like to have to attract the listed amount of money?

How can you begin today starting that business to reach the stated dream?

THE BUILDING A BETTER WORLD PYRAMID

Where Do You Fit?

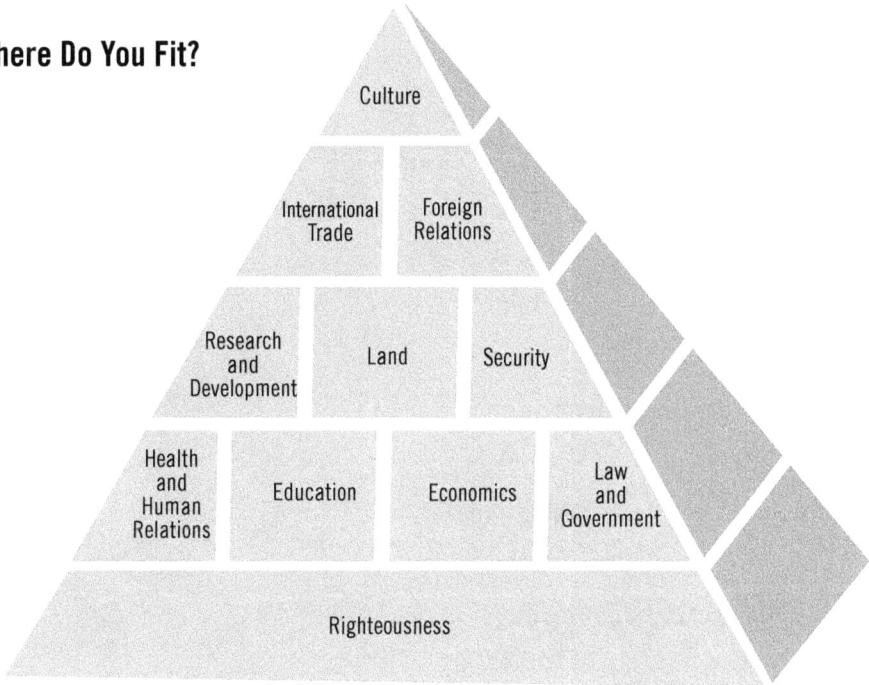

Culture

International Trade

Foreign Relations

Research and Development

Land

Security

Health and Human Relations

Education

Economics

Law and Government

Righteousness

What are the 3 boxes of the Pyramid that best match your interests and talents?

1. _____

2. _____

3. _____

What can you do to make the above listed boxes in the Pyramid a reality?

How will others benefit from you making that box a reality?

173

CONTRIBUTION AND SERVICE

How can you contribute to building a better world?

If you could change anything about your school, community, or the world, what would it be?

What can you do to make that change?

How will that change help others?

Complete this sentence: My dream is...

Does your dream benefit others?

If you are unable to describe how others would benefit from the realization of your dream, how could you rework your dream to benefit others?

Describe this dream.

What do you do well that other people do not do as well?

What unique gift and talent can you offer the world?

The year is 2350. Historians are writing about your contribution to the world. What would you like them to say?

YOUR DREAM

Do not take into consideration the costs or how reasonable your dream is. Dream an "impossible dream."

What would you do if you were guaranteed success in any activity you undertook?

What is preventing you from moving forward with that dream?

Describe your dream for your personal life:

Describe your dream for your career:

How much money would you like to earn next year?

If money were not a consideration, what would your dream be to serve humanity?

Describe the "impossible dream" that you would like to achieve:

What type of person would you like to be? Describe your desired traits:

Do you believe that you can live your dreams? If not, why not?

If yes, specifically what must you do to make your dreams a reality?

VISION AND MISSION STATEMENTS

Visualization Exercises

Sit in a quiet location.

Slow your breathing.

Relax.

Are you relaxed?

Close your eyes...

Returning to your earlier projection, visualize yourself doing what you would ideally like to be doing in one year. See the people who are around you. See the work environment. Visualize your clothes. Hear yourself talking. Spend ten minutes visualizing yourself one year from now.

Take a deep breath.

Relax.

Close your eyes again and visualize yourself doing what you would like to be doing three, ten, and twenty years from now. Spend ten minutes on each exercise.

VISION STATEMENT

Based on the visualization exercises you just completed, write a descriptive statement in vivid detail of your dream:

_____

_____

_____

_____

_____

Describe what you would do, how your environment appears, the people interacting with you, and what you are accomplishing:

_____

_____

MISSION STATEMENT

"Mission": The special task with which a person is charged.
(Source: Webster's New Collegiate Dictionary)

Your mission statement should be simple, be one sentence long, and it should inspire you.

Write the conclusion to this sentence:

Recognizing my unique talents, interests, and dream, my life's mission is…

For example, a person who feels education is his life's calling may write: "My mission is to make learning fun."

Note: Your mission statement does not necessarily have to be related to the work or activities in which you are currently involved.

RESEARCH, INFORMATION, AND KNOWLEDGE

Your dream can be developed into a project, program, or business. This project, program, or business is the model that will manifest the realization of your dream.

What information will you need to implement your dream into a project, program, or business?

List the topics that you will need to understand in order to implement your dream:

What areas do you need to know more about?

Who do you know who is knowledgeable about some aspect of your dream?

Who could advise you on your dream? (This list can include people you do not know.)

How can they be contacted?

Determine exactly what question(s) you would ask them if given the opportunity:

What books can your local school or library offer on this subject?

Which websites can offer relevant information?

CHARACTER

How would you define character?

What character traits do you admire?

What are your personal character strengths?

What areas would you like to improve?

What character traits would you like to see in others with whom you work?

SACRIFICE, FOCUS, AND PRIORITIES

What are your priorities in life?

List the activities that take up your time and how much time you spend on each.

For example:

1. Sleep – 8 hours a day
2. Internet – 2 hours
3. TV – 1 hour, 30 minutes
4. Work – 8 hours
5. Commuting – 1 hour, 45 minutes
6. Shopping – 1 hour
7. Talking on the phone – 45 minutes

What are you willing to sacrifice on the above list in order to realize your dream?

Does your time allocation reflect your priorities?

What changes would you like to make?

FAITH, OBSTACLES, AND CREATIVITY

Name three people you respect. (These can be people you know personally, or people who are famous.)

What obstacles or challenges did they face?

How did they deal with their obstacles?

What lessons can you learn from their lives as it relates to your dream's fulfillment?

What obstacles can you foresee that you may face in the process of working to realize your dream?

When faced with these potential obstacles, how can you overcome these challenges?

STRUGGLE, DETERMINATION, AND STARTING SMALL

Ten-Step Implementation Plan

Think of the fulfillment of your dream as the final destination of a journey. The starting point is determining your dream. The fulfillment of your dream is the tree. Every tree begins as a seed, it sprouts, and then grows.

What activity can you pursue *today* toward the realization of your dream?

Describe an action you can take today. This action should not be dependent on anyone else or involve anything else that you do not currently have in your possession. This action is your first point on your road map.

A "stage" of your dream would be major development points and a "step" would be any action to move the realization of a stage.

Determine 10 critical stages in the development and implementation of your dream.

1. _____
2. _____
3. _____
4. _____
5. _____
6. _____
7. _____
8. _____
9. _____
10._____

Each step consists of a simpler action that leads to the next step, with a natural progression leading to the fulfillment of one stage of your dream. You may not now have in your possession all the resources needed for all stages. Look at these key stages on your road map to realizing your dream. At each stage determine the resources—material and human—needed to make that stage a reality.

What information and knowledge will you need to bring each stage to fruition?

What problems, struggles, and obstacles can you anticipate at each stage of development?

How will you overcome these obstacles?

What state of mind will you need to be successful in this struggle?

Do you have the desire for your dream and the will to overcome obstacles?

How will you benefit by enduring and overcoming the obstacles that you are bound to face?

THE TRUNK

Taking Action

YOUR PLAN OF ACTION

Use the elements drafted previously and now incorporate them into your overall plan.

1. The Dream: a summary of your dream (completed previously)

2. Mission Statement (completed previously)

3. How this will serve others (completed previously)

4. Ten-Step Implementation Plan (completed previously)

5. Organization and Structure

    a) Legal structure (This point may not apply for all projects)

    b) Divide the project into categories that team members will have to manage

6. The Team

    a) Roles and responsibilities

    b) Assignments and dates

    c) Discuss time commitments

    d) Discuss standards

    e) Team members should share their vision of their role in the implementation of the project

    f) Decision-making procedures

    g) Conflict-resolution procedures

    h) Financial priorities and use of resources

7. Resources and Budget

    a) Identify the resources that you will need at each stage of your plan

8. Creativity

    a) If you do not get the resources and money that you would like to have, determine how to proceed without them. (For example: You may decide that you will need an office with a copier and fax machine.)

The reality is that you do not have the money for that office and the equipment. You may have to take a table in the corner of your garage or your kitchen table and declare, "This table is my office." The local photocopying store and its fax machine will become an extension of your office.

At each stage of your implementation plan, anticipate potential problems. Using your creative genius, develop plans to overcome those potential challenges.

---

9. Marketing

    a) List friends, family, and contacts who will support you

    b) Describe the type of person who would be interested in your service

    c) Where do you find such people?

    d) Determine methods of making the targeted market aware and interested in your project or business

YEAR-LONG AND MONTHLY GOALS

In writing your plan of action, you previously wrote a 10-Step Implementation Plan. Give a summary description to each stage, such as, "Research," "Planning," "Implementation."

Now, establish dates to begin and complete each of the ten development stages. The grander the dream, the more time you will need.

Stage 1:_____

From:_____   To:_____

Stage 2:_____

From:_____   To:_____

Stage 3:_____

From:_____   To:_____

Stage 4:_____

From:_____   To:_____

Stage 5:_____

From:_____   To:_____

Stage 6:_____

From:_____   To:_____

Stage 7:_____

From:_____   To:_____

Stage 8:_____

From:_____   To:_____

Stage 9:_____

From:_____   To:_____

Stage 10:_____

From:_____   To:_____

IMPLEMENTATION STEPS

"Stage" – Major road marks in the development of your dream

"Step" – Simple actions that collectively will bring the "stage" into reality

For Stage 1, list steps you will take to manifest that stage. Steps should be simple actions.

Steps 1 and 2 should be activities that you can do yourself with what you currently have at your disposal. The steps, like climbing a staircase, will often fall into a natural progression. By making each step a simple activity, there is less of a chance that you will be overwhelmed. By completing each step, you are moving toward a critical stage of your plan of action, and you are making your dream a reality.

Stage 1:_____

(Title or theme of this stage)

Implementation Time Frame:

From: _____

To: _____

Steps to Make Stage 1 a Reality:

(Use your own discretion as to how many steps you will need)

Step #1 _____

Date to Complete: _____

Step #2: _____

Date to Complete: _____

Step #3: _____

Date to Complete: _____

Step #4: _____

Date to Complete: _____

Step #5: _____

Date to Complete: _____

TIME MANAGEMENT

Life's Activities

Refer to the list of activities that you prepared for Steps to Make Stage 1 a Reality.

These steps become part of the priorities that you must complete daily or weekly, based on the time frame you have given yourself. Santa Claus will not get them done for you. They (i.e. the steps toward your dream) must be a part of your daily priorities. Getting these simple tasks done will enable you to live your dream.

Purchase a daily scheduling calendar, make your own using the model below, or use the one on your smartphone.

Complete the time management schedule.

Block out the time for established regular activities. Write a schedule that will allow you to meet your obligations and daily priorities.

Sample:

Time	Activity
12:00	Lunch
12:15	
12:30	
12:45	
1:00	Write letter for project
1:15	
1:30	
1:45	Return phone calls
2:00	Take walk
2:15	
2:30	
2:45	Drive to dry cleaners
3:00	Arrive at cleaners

SAMPLE DAY

Date:_____

Morning

6:00_____

6:15_____

6:30_____

6:45_____

7:00_____

7:15_____

7:30_____

7:45_____

8:00_____

8:15_____

8:30_____

8:45_____

9:00_____

9:15_____

9:30_____

9:45_____

10:00_____

10:15_____

10:30_____

10:45_____

11:00_____

11:15_____

11:30_____

11:45_____

Afternoon

12:00 _____

12:15_____

12:30_____

12:45_____

1:00_____

1:15_____

1:30_____

1:45_____

2:00_____

2:15_____

2:30_____

2:45_____

3:00_____

3:15_____

3:30_____

3:45_____

4:00_____

4:15_____

4:30_____

4:45_____

5:00_____

5:15_____

5:30_____

5:45_____

Evening

6:00 _____

6:15 _____

6:30 _____

6:45 _____

7:00 _____

7:15 _____

7:30 _____

7:45 _____

8:00 _____

8:15 _____

8:30 _____

8:45 _____

9:00 _____

9:15 _____

9:30 _____

9:45 _____

10:00 _____

10:15 _____

10:30 _____

10:45 _____

11:00 _____

11:15 _____

11:30 _____

11:45 _____

12:00 Midnight

RESOURCES

What do you need to get started on your dream?

How can you utilize any of the following? List the ways you use them as a resource:

- School

- Internet

- Library

- People

- Other

Is there a lack of resources that will prevent you from getting started?

If so, what can you do to replace them in order to move forward despite not having all that you need?

THE BRANCHES

Building Your Dream

TEAMWORK

With whom would you like to work on your project? Name specific people.

What skills and traits do you need in your team members?

What qualities do you want to avoid?

What specific tasks and responsibilities do you need team members to carry out?

Discuss with team members your goals, time frame, and level of commitment that you expect from them.

Discuss conflict resolution and decision-making procedures.

Draft an agreement of how the team as a whole will function with individual roles and responsibilities.

HUMAN RELATIONS

Success will often come through the people you know and meet. People are one of your most important resources. Organize this resource in the following ways:

(1) Digitally organize friends, relatives, school contacts, and other relevant categories.

In addition to contact information, list their line of work, where you met them, spouse's or secretary's name, and any other relevant information.

HEALTH

Exercise

Your Height   Your Weight:

Which statement best describes your exercise routine: (Circle one)

1. Poor – I hate to exercise, but I do run to the kitchen during every commercial.

2. Fair – I am not in good shape, but I firmly believe in exercise and one day I will…

3. Average – I exercise whenever I can, and I could afford to lose a couple of pounds.

4. Very Good – I exercise regularly. Generally, I eat a healthy diet.

5. Excellent – Yesterday I worked on my pecs and lats, tomorrow calves, and I never eat fast food.

Do you currently have a workout program?

If you do not exercise, list activities that would be easy for you start doing this week:

If yes, do you enjoy it?

If not, what can you do to make it fun or what other activities could you do that you enjoy more?

For those who do exercise, what can you do to improve your level of conditioning to one level higher on the scale listed above?

List four things you can (and will actually do) to improve your conditioning and overall health.

1. _____

2. _____

3. _____

4. _____

(Try tackling one item at a time.)

For those not working out regularly, list three activities that you would do and enjoy as a form of exercise (for example, walking on the beach or bowling with friends).

1. _____

2. _____

3. _____

NOTE: In the "Time Management" section of this workbook, plan time to exercise.

DIET

Which statement best describes your diet: (Circle one)

1. Poor – Is ketchup a vegetable?

2. Fair – I am cutting back on fats and junk.

3. Average – I eat a well-balanced diet.

4. Very Good – I eat lots of fruits and veggies, a little red meat, but I do enjoy sweets on occasion.

5. Excellent – Today I will have a spinach salad with a glass of carrot juice–organic, of course.

Name four actions you can take that would improve your diet:

1. _____

2. _____

3. _____

4. _____

Implement one of the above listed actions today.

MENTAL STRESS AND RELAXATION

Which best describes the level of stress in your life: (Circle one)

1. Low
2. Moderate
3. Occasional
4. Stressful
5. Intense

How do you relieve stress?

How often do you do this stress-relief activity?

What can you do in the future to reduce your level of stress?

FUN

What do you do for fun?

How often do you do this?

What would you like to do for fun, but never or rarely get to do?

What can you do to be able to do this activity?

Make time to have fun!

How to Live Your Dreams

FRIENDS

In your time-management schedule, make time to call and be with friends.

Invite your friends over and share your life stories and your dreams.

Challenge your friends to live their dream by finding their trees and getting started.

How can you and your friends work to support each other in pursuing your dreams?

ORGANIZATION AND LEADERSHIP

Describe the traits that you admire in an effective leader:

Do you have any of these traits?

What can you do to develop your leadership skills?

What are your strengths as a leader?

What areas of leadership do you need to improve upon?

What traits do you need in others to best complement your strengths and weaknesses?

How can you structure your team so that each person's strength is utilized?

203

EXCELLENCE

Failure: What a Blessing

List past activities or projects at which you failed or performed poorly:

What did you learn from these failures?

What would you do differently if you were to do them again?

List struggles you have had in your life:

Looking back, what did you learn from these challenges?

What has prevented you from achieving your goals in the past?

What can you do now to overcome those obstacles?

"Details make the difference."
—John Wooden

What details will make the difference in producing excellence in your project, program, or business?

How can you make sure these details are implemented to perfection?

MUSIC

What is the theme song for your life as you live your dream?

Select or write your song:

LITERATURE

Write the story of your life (as you would like it to happen) after you started living your dream:

INTERNATIONAL RELATIONS

What culture or area in the world fascinates you?

Why?

Do you know anyone from there?

Do you know where you can find out more information about that place or culture?

Are there clubs, organizations, or events representing that region or culture in your area (e.g., art exhibits, cultural events, or restaurants)?

Go to an event, museum, or restaurant that represents the culture or area of the world that fascinates you.

Meet people from there and let people know that you want to travel there one day.

Meet someone from that region, and ask if he or she knows someone with whom you could connect with on Facebook.

Contact that person.

Go online and find out how much it will cost for a flight there.

Write the price here:

Use the Internet to find out about housing possibilities, whether in a hotel or youth hostel.

Write the cost here:

Determine when you will go.

How much money can you save each week toward your trip?

Find a can and start saving.

Go to your dream destination.

THE FRUIT

Starting Your Business

ECONOMICS

Your Business

How can you turn your gift and talents into a business?

How can recipients benefit from your service or product?

Describe the type of person who would be interested in what you have to offer.

MONEY

How much money would you like to earn next year?

How many products would you have to sell or how much service would you have to provide to reach that goal?

This section will outline the basic steps to start your own business.

In order to reach the sales total listed above, you will need a plan of action—a business plan.

CUSTOMERS AND MARKET RESEARCH

Describe the type of person that you expect to be your customer. Will your customers be children, teenagers, or adults?

Age Range: From   years to   years

Do you expect more males or females to be your customers?

What income range would your prospective customers fall into?

What type of occupation would your typical customer have?

Are there any types of organizations or activities that your customers would probably be involved in?

What businesses do you know that are already in this same line of work?

What makes them successful?

How could they improve?

How will your business differ from or be similar to your competitors?

Why would a customer choose your business over a competitor?

Develop a questionnaire that will allow you to ask people what they are looking for in a business like yours.

SERVICE AND PRODUCTS

Describe your service or product.

Are there related businesses that you can develop as your business grows?

START-UP AND THE LAW

Business Structure

- Sole Proprietorship – There is one owner. You are your own boss. You make the money, but you also have to address the problems. If there are debts, creditors can sue for your personal assets as well as those belonging to the company.

- Partnership – You share the profits and the problems. Write a partnership agreement. This agreement will outline who has to do what, who is responsible for what decision, and even how you divide the assets and debts should you close the business. This document is your "prenuptial agreement." Of course, all is wonderful in the beginning. Beware. A detailed partnership agreement can be useful should problems arise.

- LLC (Limited Liability Company) – An LLC is a popular and easy-to-form business structure that combines the liability protection of a corporation and the flexibility of a partnership.

- S-Corporation – This is a corporation with a limited number of shareholders.

- Corporation – Your business becomes its own entity. If there are debts or lawsuits, the corporation is the target, not your personal assets. This arrangement is more expensive and can involve a lawyer, unless you are comfortable with a do-it-yourself kit.

Business Licenses

These can be acquired at your local city hall.

Business Bank Account (Doing Business As, or DBA)

1. Register with your city or county registrar.
2. Place an ad in a local newspaper announcing that you are doing business under your new business's name.
3. Open a bank account under your business's name.

MARKETING

Quality

By providing quality goods and excellent service, your business will grow. Customers will refer their friends to you if you are good at what you do.

Standards

Everything you do is marketing—from how you answer the phone, what you choose as the business name, to the quality of paper you use for stationery. Everything about your business tells prospective customers about you and what they can expect. The best does not always mean the most expensive. Be meticulous and strive for excellence. Customers will notice.

Enthusiasm

Your enthusiasm for your business is your best promotion. Be enthusiastic, and customers will look forward to doing business with you. Your enthusiasm, coupled with excellent goods and service, will make your customers enthusiastic, and they will help promote your business by telling their friends.

Business Cards

Hand them out wherever you go. Make your graphics reflect the image you want for yourself and your business.

Graphics

A talented graphics artist can make your in-home business look like a major corporation.

Giveaways

Work with other businesses and give away products that will promote your business. The local high school or club can raffle off one of your products. Your business is promoted, and the organization gets a great prize.

Customer Records, Follow Up, and Repeat Business

Keep track of your customers and keep in touch for future business. Email them coupons and reminders.

Website and Online Marketing

Websites can vary in price and quality. If funds are short, consider contacting a college computer science department for students looking to build a portfolio.

Establish your online presence with YouTube, Facebook, and other relevant sites.

FINANCE AND ACCOUNTING

Make a budget of what you need in order to get started.

Make a timeline of your monetary needs.

Figure out creative ways to reduce costs.

Can you barter your services or products?

How much will you charge for your product or service?

Project the amount of income you expect to earn for three, six, and twelve months.

Calculate your cost during the same three, six, and twelve month time period.

Determine at what point will you make a profit.

Make adjustments in costs or sales goals, if possible, to meet your overall goals.

HUMAN RESOURCES

Where will you need assistance?

Find people who have talents that complement your strengths and weaknesses.

Create a "Win-Win" situation for all.

Find A Tree

12 years old

Dream…

then find a tree and get started.

Act in the spirit of service,

and despite the obstacles
and struggles,
you will be successful.

Daniel Armstrong

NOTES

About the Author

Daniel Armstrong, inspired by his experiences in Ghana, West Africa, wrote the first edition of *How to Live Your Dreams: Find a Tree and Get Started* in 1999. Subsequently, he developed the Find A Tree program and workbook to help others realize their dreams. Armstrong, a Ford Foundation Fellow who has a Juris Doctorate in law and a Master of Business Administration degree, both from UCLA, worked for two years in Ghana helping youth to improve their communities and establish their own businesses. Armstrong received his Bachelor of Arts degree in Political Science from Columbia University in New York City.

Armstrong has worked as an entrepreneur in Ghana, Zimbabwe, and the United States.

He was born and raised in Compton, California.

DREAM. LEARN. ACT. ENGAGE. MOTIVATE. INSPIRE. EXCEL. ACHIEVE. TRANSFORM. NOW.

FINDATREE.COM

www.ingramcontent.com/pod-product-compliance
Lightning Source LLC
Chambersburg PA
CBHW060027100426
42740CB00010B/1632